Who's The Girl In The Mirror?
REVISITED

> *A COLLECTION AND REFLECTION OF STORIES FROM MY PAST*

Carolyn West Reaves

Author's Tranquility Press
ATLANTA, GEORGIA

Copyright © 2023 by Carolyn West Reaves

All rights reserved. No part of this publication may be reproduced, distributed, or transmitted in any form or by any means, including photocopying, recording, or other electronic or mechanical methods, without the prior written permission of the publisher, except in the case of brief quotations embodied in critical reviews and certain other noncommercial uses permitted by copyright law. For permission requests, write to the publisher, addressed "Attention: Permissions Coordinator," at the address below.

Carolyn West Reaves/Author's Tranquility Press
3800 Camp Creek Pkwy SW Bldg. 1400-116 #1255
Atlanta, GA 30331, USA
www.authorstranquilitypress.com

Ordering Information:
Quantity sales. Special discounts are available on quantity purchases by corporations, associations, and others. For details, contact the "Special Sales Department" at the address above.

Who's The Girl In The Mirror? Revisited/Carolyn West Reaves
Paperback: 978-1-962492-67-6
eBook: 978-1-962492-68-3

Table of Contents

INTRODUCTION i
THE MIRROR 1
SCHOOL YEARS 3
A DREAM 11
MONSTERS 13
JOURNEYS IMAGINED 15
UNCOMFORTABLE DINNER GUEST 17
JOURNEY AND ADVENTURE WITH THE PERKINS 19
COUSINS AND OTHER KIN FOLK... 23
IMAGINATION STATION... 25
NO SHOES, NO POLISH, NO PROBLEM 27
CHOOSE YOUR BATTLES 29
HAIRDOS I WILL NEVER FORGET 30
HELP BUT DO NOT HINDER 33
WRESTLING WITH A BEAST IN THE WASHING MACHINE 34
FOODS I NEVER WANT TO EAT AGAIN 35
THE CRACKER JACK SURPRISE... 37
CLEANING UP WHEN YOU DON'T HAVE A BATHROOM IN THE HOUSE 38
THE NEED FOR MORE THAN A PATH 39
NEEDING NEW SHOES... 40
CATCHING CHICKENS...41
GRANDMA AND THE BISCUIT EATING NEIGHBOR 43
CHARLES' TALE ABOUT CHRISTMAS GIFTS.......................... 45
HALLOWEEN AND NOT TRICK OR TREATING 47
LOOKING FOR A CHRISTMAS TREE 49
PICKING BLACKBERRIES 51
PAGEANTS 53

GATHER NO DUST	56
MOVING UP THE CHICKEN CHAIN	57
UNFORGETTABLE FUNERALS	58
GOING TO THE DOGS	60
LEARNING TO SEW	64
DATING, PORCH LIGHTS, AND GETTING MARRIED	66
DEATH BY CANCER	71
PAINTING FOR CHURCHES	83
JASON- SUICIDE WAS REAL	85
DAD'S CONVERSATION ABOUT BLACK STAR	90
A CALL TO SERVE	92
SPECIAL PEOPLE WE HAVE MET AT CHURCHES	101
DINNER WITH A STRANGER	103
CONVERSATION WITH DAD	118
Fall to Winter	121
Dealing With Loss	122
Between Life and Death	123
The Face	124
I Remember	125
Think for Today	126
Spring on its Way	127
My Dad and How He Lived	128
MY FAMILY	129
QUARANTINED AND FACING A FUNERAL	134
ACKNOWLEDGEMENT	136

INTRODUCTION

I never envisioned that I would one day write a book, but so many thoughts, events, and facts started to come to my memory. I want my children, grandchildren, and great-grandchildren to appreciate where they came from, and it just seemed natural. We have taken numerous pictures but haven't always left a story about what was going on the day the picture was taken. I hope this book will give others a look at me and my family and they will come to know us better.

It is my hope that my children will respect me, and the guidelines I gave them for life. I hope all the memories of good times will overshadow all the dark times, and that a brighter day will come. I want them to know that God loves them, not because any of us deserves it, but because he didn't wait until we deserved it to die for us. He loves us all, just as we are, even in our sin.

Hopefully, this book will show that no matter how dark your pathway seems, there is light at the end of that tunnel. You can't give up; you need to learn from your mistakes or even the mistakes of others. We are not perfect and never will be until we reach heaven. As Christ forgave each of us, we must learn to forgive those that do not treat us fairly, even those that treat us as if we are disgusting and evil. Even if they do not ask for forgiveness, forgive them, and let it go. There is nothing in this world that is worth more than the love of God. He sees each of us at our best, even if others do not agree.

If you know Jesus as your personal savior, you have all you need to get through this world and have a hope of heaven. Nothing more is required. If you feel that tugging in your heart to accept the Lord, He is always there, waiting for you to come to Him. His love covered a multitude of sins, and He is always listening, even when your world seems dark and unkind. Your heart communicates with God when your voice doesn't seem to know how to put the words together. What are you waiting for? He offers you peace and contentment.

THE MIRROR

Getting a glimpse of myself in a mirror, I often wondered what others saw when they looked at me. I knew when I looked at my reflection and saw my parted hair, always on the right, it reflected exactly the opposite of how it really was. As a child, I would think about this and wonder if I really looked to other people like I saw myself. The shiny reflection didn't always show who I really was. Outward appearances deceived those that I came into contact with. I would wonder about things concerning my future. I also watched my dad comb his hair and his part showed him to look different in that mirror than he did in real life.

I would click around in my Aunt Eula Smith's high heels when we visited her, pretending I was a grown woman. When I looked into the mirror, I saw myself much older than three or four years old and I felt powerful looking at that reflection. I remember everyone laughing as I came through the house clip-clopping in those shoes and pretending my dolls were my children. I never quit trying to be that woman everyone would notice, not for what I looked like, but what I did for others. It was not to get recognition, but to be helpful to others in need.

At that young age, when I looked in the mirror, after giving myself a haircut, I saw myself as fearless, only for a moment. The mirror didn't have to say anything; I just felt the rush of having conquered a giant when I looked at the new me in that mirror. I only felt this way for a short time as my mom came in shortly after I had practiced a few major snips in my hair. This was definitely a life-changing experience for me.

The mirror always watched me, and at times I wished it would not be so intrusive. It still points out the blemishes, gray hair, and extra weight that I certainly didn't want to see, but all my faults are there anyway, just as they were, even as a child. I never really liked how I looked at myself or how I thought others saw me.

The mirror of my soul is a reflection of what I believe, what I feel, and how I treat others. It reflects out to those I come into contact with.

The mirror may seem to be tarnished at times when I feel battered, and I want to look away and find a better state of mind. Bright light makes the reflection shine differently. Rumors, lies and just un-Christian behavior from those related closely to me make the look change to bitterness at times. Attitudes can change and should be checked often.

When I shop for clothes, I sometimes remember a time when people would make fun of my clothes and my hair. Their eyes were my mirror. I didn't like the way they made me feel, and I told myself I would remember those images and work hard to improve that when I could. I now think no matter how I feel, I need to get up, get dressed, show up, and try to never give up.

The mirrors of the soul sometimes need to be cleaned to show a reflection of what I really am, not what others think they see. All the feelings of inadequacy and feeling unloved at times come back when people show disrespect and are not pleasing to God.

Mirror, Mirror in my life,
Can you help me with this strife? For so long I've tried my best.
Is this real or only a test?

—Carolyn Reaves

Psalms 119:37—*Turn away mine eyes from beholding vanity; and quicken thou me in thy way.*

SCHOOL YEARS

I still remember my first day of school at Jellico Creek Elementary School, just outside of Williamsburg, Kentucky. My teacher was Ms. Minnie Chambers. She was a thin woman with gray hair and glasses. She wore sweaters of gray wool over her calico print dresses and had a voice that was seasoned from many years of teaching. She had been my mother's first-grade teacher, too. I was excited about going to school because my older sister, Louise, had already been to school for two years and I loved trying to do her homework. She would have an assignment that required memorization of a poem and I would learn the poem right along with her. I remember reciting the poem and my sister would get frustrated because she thought I was catching on to the poem faster than she was. My mother would make me do something else to occupy my time while she worked with my sister.

School was easy for me. No kindergarten classes were held in my school back then. My classroom had two grades in one room. The first-grade students sat at long tables with tiny folding wooden chairs. The second-grade students sat in rows of small desks attached to a long sled-runner type platform. As the class started each day, I recall seeing beautiful chalk drawings done on the blackboard by the teacher. She obviously worked on these before we got there, or after everyone left the day before. I remember a turkey she illustrated on the board before Thanksgiving and each tail feather seemed unique yet became a vital part of the picture. The texture was shown by blending the colors and adding detail. I was hooked on this visual part of the school. She also folded strips of newspaper accordion style, cut away some of the side areas, and made a chain of girls and boys all holding hands, that became a bulletin board border. I watched her and could hardly wait to go home and see if I could make the same kind of chain of boys and girls.

I loved to draw and work with my hands, and I recall making a paste with flour and water and making chains from strips of construction paper. The glue had a sour smell after a couple of days and had to be used quickly because it didn't last like the commercial glues one buys today. I learned to read well but wanted to draw more than I wanted to read. The teacher would punish me for drawing when I was supposed to be reading. That same chalkboard that held the beautiful illustrations would have a circle drawn on it, by the teacher, and I would be escorted to the board to stand with my nose in the chalk-ring for a time which seemed like an eternity. Nothing could have been worse to me than having to go to the chalk-ring and face my punishment.

By Christmas, I had already read all of the books required for the first year of school and would have been double promoted, but my father had decided to move to Michigan to find work. I was not double promoted but read the same books that I had already read in Kentucky. The move was terrifying for me, but I adjusted well. My first teacher in Michigan was Ms. Emma Dame. The school was Maple Grove School. The classroom had more modern looking desks that had a hinged lid that allowed you to prop the desk up for lunch and down for schoolwork. We had no lunchroom and brought our lunch in metal lunch boxes or paper bags and bought milk at school. The milk was delivered to our classroom at lunchtime in little glass bottles with a paper fastened on top of them. I remember the smell of Ms. Dame's coffee as she poured it from her thermos and used a bit of the bottled milk to suit her taste.

One thing about the Michigan classroom that made the classroom special for me was the art center that was available to each student as they finished their classwork. There were no ditto sheets; just blank Manila paper waiting to be painted or colored. Scissors and glue were also available. I made books about many things. I would illustrate the books and staple several pages together to complete the book. This free expression was great and helped me to feel good about going to school. I never had to put my nose in the chalk-ring again.

At the end of the school year, I was promoted to second grade, and I had the pleasure of having Ms. Dame for my second-grade teacher. She divided the classroom into small groups for reading orally. We sat in a small corner of the room in a circle and took turns reading. The reading groups were named interesting names: satellites, jets, and rockets. The rockets were the top readers in the room and the satellites were those that needed more help. We read from different reading books and looked forward to the time of the day devoted to reading. The names were selected due to the fact that Science was a major focus in education, and this was the time of Sputnik. Weekly Readers were ordered for each student and students were asked to take the sheets home for family discussion. I loved taking this home as my dad even liked to read them with me.

We never took vacations like many other people. The only trip I ever recall was when we traveled from Michigan to Kentucky to visit our grandparents. The trip was always long, and we never stopped getting a bite to eat. The only stops dad would make were to get gas so we could get back on the road. One time, I remember waking up while we were traveling, and Louise was drinking a bottle of Grapette Soda. I asked her where she had gotten it and she told me, "You were asleep when dad stopped to get gas, so you didn't get one." She was right about that. I didn't get one and I was again left out, even in my own family. That is how things went for me much of my life. I either got left out, had to take what was picked out for me, or wore the hand-me-downs that somebody else wore.

I finished first and second grade in Michigan and began third grade. It was a hot September and dad wanted to move because work was not steady, and he longed to be back with family in Kentucky. I was sick with something they called Hepatitis. I was deathly ill and even though I was only almost eight years old, I still remember how yellow I was, how nauseated I was, and how my body had no control over any of its functions. I sweated and then I would freeze. I couldn't get to the bathroom fast enough and I would have to change clothes and take a bath. It was the worst I have ever felt in my life. I couldn't go to school and dad was out of work. There was no health insurance, and I had no desire to get better. That is a bad state to be in when you are a child.

Mom took me to our family doctor in Michigan. The doctor wanted to put me in the hospital, but mom told them we didn't have health insurance. As she was paying the bill, I remember passing out in the reception area and the nurse came out and helped get me back into one of the rooms. Mom and dad were planning to move back to Kentucky, so she took me back home and I just suffered while they packed.

Dad moved us back to Kentucky as he was out of work and had a hope of finding work "back home". On the way there, I began craving cold things because I was sick. I remember dad griping because mom needed to get some food and he didn't have much money. He stopped at a small convenience store and mom let me go in with her to see what I thought I could eat. I saw store-bought red gelatin and it looked like something I might keep down. It was cold and I only wanted something cold. She bought it, even though she said I probably wouldn't eat it. She insisted I better try if she bought it.

I tried eating the gelatin and it was not what I needed. I started throwing up and then dad was mad because I had her to buy the gelatin and it was wasted. Money gone was not we needed right now, but I was not making this sickness up in my head. I felt awful because I could not make myself better. I really was extremely sick.

We made it to Kentucky, but the moving van got lost, and we didn't see our furniture for two solid weeks. All we had at their old farmhouse was a porch swing, an old white kitchen table, a mattress on the floor, a refrigerator, and a kitchen stove. I was given the privilege of sleeping on the mattress because I was sick, and everyone thought I was getting ready to die. Even I thought this and didn't care about getting well anymore. Mom finally took me to a doctor in Williamsburg called Dr. Clinton. He was married to a Native American woman, and she had a long braid at the back of her head. His advice to my mom was to give me tablespoons of clear Karo syrup with nothing else. I was about too weak to stand up and I lost about twenty pounds. I was severely dehydrated. It was hard to swallow the syrup, but this gave me enough energy to start moving around and have an appetite. This went on for a month. I missed the first month of third grade due to this illness.

One evening in late September, I remember mom and dad were outside cleaning up some weeds and doing yard work. I was sitting on the old rock step that used to be at the back of the house. I began craving food. Actually, I wanted some bacon. When mom came back to the house, I told her what I thought I could eat. She was so excited that I was getting an appetite back, she immediately began making the bacon. She burned the bacon, but I ate it and it stayed down. I was now on the road to recovery.

When I went back to school, there were three grades in one classroom, and it was a noisy place. I remember how the school smelled and how the children looked back then. The school was old and hadn't really changed its appearance much in a couple of years we were away.

I got finished with that year and started fourth grade in another classroom with 5th grade also in that room. The teacher told me I had better handwriting than she did and would let me write things on the chalkboard for her. This was motivation enough for me to try really hard to do a good job in this teacher's room. Her name was Mrs. Gladys Meadors. We studied a unit about the early way of travel, and she had me to draw a poster of a covered wagon. I also had this teacher for 5th grade, and I enjoyed the hands-on learning again in her room as she had me draw a poster drawing of our elementary school. My mom took a picture of me holding that poster. The poster was part of a display in Williamsburg highlighting and informing about our school. It was displayed in a storefront on Main Street of our little town. Our whole school was involved in the project. My younger brother Ralph did a written document that was also part of the display. I have no pictures of that little school, but I have a picture of me holding the poster at home before it was presented to the teachers.

Sixth grade was blended with Seventh and Eighth grades in one classroom, and Mrs. Letha Taylor was our teacher. She was a very good teacher and had us doing lots of research about birds and making poetry books. We did lots of memorization work, too. I remember she had us to memorize the Preamble to the Constitution, the Lord's Prayer, and many poems by Robert Frost and Sara Teasdale.

We made pictures to hang on the bulletin board. I remember in her windowsills; she had some artificial orange trumpet vines that looked real. They looked so real that the hummingbirds would come to the window and try to get to the flowers. That school prepared me for high school and for my desire to go to college later on.

High School was filled with many opportunities, and I experienced a lot of new classes that primed me for going to college and for decisions regarding a major focus. I especially liked home economics classes and art classes. I could do things without having to do talking very much and I had something to take home that I was proud of. I always sewed clothes for Diane and Pam when I had to make a home project. Their clothes didn't require as much fabric and they needed new clothes, too. As I graduated high school, I started thinking more about college. I wanted to major in home economics, but the closest school that offered that major was Eastern Kentucky University, in Richmond, KY. Mom told me if I went to college I had to go to Cumberland or I couldn't go to college. It was close by, and I could get a ride to school with my dad or others coming to college from that direction. When I started into college, Louise had already completed her sophomore year. She was riding with her boyfriend, referred to by his initials, H.C., and James Lee Meadors. That became my ride for a year. I then had to ride with dad and had to wait for him until around 5:00PM, carrying my books and art supplies with me all day because I had no car to put them in.

I had taken driver's training in high school, and learned to drive well, but mom wouldn't let me get my driver's license because she didn't want to add me to the insurance. Jerry turned sixteen and I was a junior in college, age nineteen and I still didn't have a car. He got to buy a Mustang and get his license because he was a boy. I never said anything about it, even though it did hurt my feelings. I was toughened by all the treatment I got. I got my license, and I was determined that I would eventually get a car of my own. I finished college in three years and got married a couple of months after graduation.

Into my fifth year of teaching, schooling was to begin on my master's degree program. I enrolled and began working on that at Union College in Barbourville, KY as that was the closest school that offered the master's program at that time. I did additional graduate work there related to my career and completed 80 graduate hours there with additional endorsements in principalship, supervisor of schools, and superintendent training. After retirement from the public schools. I again started another degree. I was a member of the first cohort to graduate with a Doctor of Education degree, in 2011, at the University of the Cumberlands, formerly Cumberland College. That had been on my list of things to do for quite some time. I could hardly believe I finished it when I did. During that same time frame, I was given a distinguished honor of Kentucky Colonel. This award is a special one that is based upon good character and recognition by another Kentucky Colonel.

Proverbs 1:7—*The fear of the LORD [is] the beginning of knowledge: [but] fools despise wisdom.*

A DREAM

My dreams were not as vivid as my imagination during my waking hours. I do recall a dream I had when I was very young.

I dreamed my family had gone to visit my Aunt Morna and Uncle Harold. They lived just up the road from us. It was a breezy day and would have been a great day to fly a kite. Their younger children, Joan and June, were about the same age as my sister and me. My dream started out in their yard, playing in the wind, and trying to keep from splashing in a huge mudhole in their yard. They always seemed to have that huge mudhole. As I got to the mudhole, my feet suddenly left the ground and I found myself flying across the house and enjoying the freedom of being above the trees and looking at what remained on the earth below.

My sister and cousins were yelling for me to come back down, but I just wanted to keep flying. In my dream, I kept flying until I could no longer hear any noise of the children in the yard, the cows in the pasture, or the dogs barking at me as they had when I left the ground. The silence was deafening in a way that I still recall so vividly yet did not understand in the dream.

I finally came back to earth to find nobody in the yard. I wondered where they were and started to panic. When I woke up, I saw my sister was asleep next to me in the bed. I got up and I immediately had this feeling that I could really fly. It was so strong that I tried to fly by flapping my arms and really concentrating on flying when I went outside, but nothing happened. I was thinking,

"If I really can fly, I will change my circumstances." I soon realized I had been dreaming. I had to stay where I was, for the time being.

Daniel 4:5— *I saw a dream and it made me fearful; and these fantasies as I lay on my bed and the visions in my mind kept alarming me.*

MONSTERS

In the Spring, at night, when I was about three, we would go to bed with the windows open. Back then, people didn't have to fear people that seem to be preying on the innocent. The sheer curtains would move when a breeze made them float away from the side of the windowpane. The noise of the night birds, the Whippoorwills, would be loud and echo through the trees. I was afraid of the sound as it was so unusual. I would lie in my bed, next to my older sister, Louise, and be very still so the noisy "monsters" would not hear me breathing. My iron bed had a design on the headboard that looked like a monster to me, too. That bed was brown and with the moonlight shining into my room, I could see the outline of the image.

I never heard the noise during the daylight hours, nor in any season except early spring. Needless to say, my sleep was often disturbed. I expected that headboard to burst open any minute and take me away. That never happened, and by the time summer rolled around, I had lived through another season of hearing the scary noise.

After Anthony and I married, his job at American Greetings in Corbin, KY was on night shift. We had been blessed with two small daughters. Angelina was always afraid of monsters that she thought lurked under her bed. I came up with a way to help her to go to sleep. I took a can of pleasant-smelling air freshener, sprayed it into areas under her bed and told her it was "Monster Spray", and as long as she could still smell the fragrance, the spray was still keeping the monsters away. By the time the fragrance had left her bedroom, she was asleep. Sometimes, it is the small things we do that make a big difference in our lives. It worked for her, and I know I slept better, too.

Isaiah 41:10—*Fear thou not; for I [am] with thee: be not dismayed; for I [am] thy God: I will strengthen thee; yea, I will help thee; yea, I will uphold thee with the right hand of my righteousness.*

JOURNEYS IMAGINED

That pine tree in the front yard seemed so tall when I was just a small child. I hadn't even started school and I remember hearing a poem about "going up in the air in a swing so high" and I would think about that poem as I soared through the air on the swing my dad made for me. The swing was made from a scrap piece of wood and ropes tied to the tops of some branches.

I also imagined I was going on a journey every time I sat on the seat of that swing and started swinging my feet back-and-forth. My journeys were limited because I had never been anywhere except when we moved to Michigan from Kentucky, and I was too young to remember the trip. I only could think of things I had seen. I-75 had not yet made its way to Kentucky, so my journeys were always on backroads then. I kept those memories to myself and never even imagined I would one day write about them in a book.

I remember wearing some of my mom's old high-heeled shoes and killing a tiny ground snake that came to crawl in the loose dirt underneath the swing one day. I wasted no time stepping on the little snake until I knew it was dead. I went inside and had my mom come out to see what I had just killed with my shoes. I told her it was a big worm.

Mom looked at me and said, "That isn't a worm; that's a snake!" She was startled that I killed the snake by repeatedly stomping it with my shoes instead of running inside to get her. I guess I felt I should face the giants all by myself some of the time.

Jeremiah 29:11—*For I know the thoughts that I think toward you, saith the LORD, thoughts of peace, and not of evil, to give you an expected end.*

UNCOMFORTABLE DINNER GUEST

It was in the early fall season, in Trenton, Michigan. The long, hot summer was coming to an end and school had already started. My sister was in the fourth grade, and I was in the second grade. We never really went anywhere except to school through the week, occasionally to the grocery store, and church on Sunday. We usually stayed in our own yard and had very few friends in our neighborhood.

The church we attended was a small Baptist church that met in an old theater building with theater seats for the congregation to sit on. We never went to any other denomination except the Baptist church. One day, my sister Louise got to bring one of her friends home to visit and have dinner with us. It was on a Friday evening, and we could watch television and just have fun. After a couple of hours, her older brother came by to pick her up.

My mom had fixed hotdogs and all the trimmings for supper. Typically, this was a meal we enjoyed. The visiting guest would not eat the hot dog and we didn't know why. She said she was not allowed. When her brother came over, he explained that it was because she was Catholic, and she was not allowed to eat this meat on Friday. My mom felt so embarrassed for not fixing something that she could enjoy, but mom didn't have any way of knowing until it was too late. This gave us all a lesson in treating others with humility and also encouraged us to find out if there were any food that needed to be avoided in the future. It made it hard for any of us to partake of the meal because we didn't want to offend the guest. I guess this lesson was meant to be learned, but we never expected to learn it this way.

Hebrews 13:9— *For it is a good thing that the heart be established with grace; not with meats, which have not profited them that have been occupied therein.*

JOURNEY AND ADVENTURE WITH THE PERKINS

I remember my Grandpa Perkins had an old car that I could barely see outside of the window. The car was old and I was only about three or four at the time. I could tell when we were getting close to the Bethel Church in McCreary County, KY by seeing the tall treetops. I remember seeing the church when we got there. It was just a short drive from their house, and we didn't get to stay with them very often, so it was always fun. I still remember the piano at that church had a mirror that reflected the keys as the pianist played for the choir. It was fascinating to me. After church, we would go back to Grandma and Grandpa's house where Grandma would cook some lunch.

She would sometimes slice bananas and put them between vanilla wafers for us for dessert, and I thought it was a special treat. Grandma cooked with propane gas, and I remember Aunt Velma roasting marshmallows for us, with a fork over the open flame. That was also a special treat. Simple things are often the best. Every time I make a banana pudding, I think of those days.

Grandma and Grandpa Perkins had a fishpond on their farm, and it was fun to go out and dig around for fish bait that we could use to fish at the pond. Grandpa eventually had a devoted fish bait area in the backyard, that he fed with coffee grounds. I remember one time that we were there, Grandma caught a fish, and when she removed it from the hook, that fish had swallowed another fish. I had never seen that happen before. Grandma, Louise, and I caught enough fish for a meal, and she cooked them for our lunch.

Grandma Perkins would make oatmeal to put in Grandpa's lunch. No microwaves were invented, yet, and I wondered how he managed to eat it after it had gotten cold, but evidently, he liked it that way.

Grandpa had a way of staring at you that would make you think you were doing something wrong. At the dinner table, everything would be quiet, and Grandpa would just be watching you eat. It would make me drop my fork, sometimes. He might ask things like, "Are those your own teeth?" Of course, I couldn't say, "Well yes, why do you ask?" I would just answer politely "yes, or no", depending on the question. The staring would continue as he watched me eat my meal.

The Perkins and Douglas side of the family were all musical. Every Christmas would be special when all the family would gather in the living room to sing around the old pump organ. Aunt Genny played the organ and taught me how to play, "What a Friend We have in Jesus", on that organ. They all sang different parts and made very good harmony. Great Uncle Earl Douglas, my grandmother's brother, would usually come over to visit and he loved to sing, too. It seems strange to recall all those that are no longer with us. The music has stopped playing and the voices are no longer making melody here on earth but, in heaven, they are having the best time of their life, I believe.

It would especially be memorable when our cousins would be visiting from Ohio. We could always find something to do at that little farm. In the front yard, they had some very tall Oak trees. The leaves would be everywhere in the fall. We would pile the leaves up in huge piles and cover each other up and play a game like, "Rise Up Dead Man".

Grandpa liked to have a pony for plowing his garden and he would have the pony trained to do things such as bowing down on its front legs when he told us it was going to pray. Grandpa was probably the "Pony Whisperer" to his grandkids. He had an old sled that he could hook up to the old horse or mule and give us a ride.

When I was in first grade in Michigan, I remember we came home to visit one weekend and I was supposed to do a leaf collection for school. Grandpa Perkins and I, along with Louise and Jerry, went into the woods across the road from his house and gathered lots of different kinds of leaves. I remember how he carefully took toothpicks and threaded the leaves onto notebook paper for me and told me what kind of leaves they were. I was amazed at how many different leaves he could recognize just from looking at them. Grandpa worked at a lumber company, so he was very familiar with timber and trees. He also found huge hickory nuts in that wooded area for us that day. I don't remember ever seeing any that large since then. I remember listening for squirrels and even seeing some in the tall trees and recognizing what a squirrel nest looked like in a tree. I recall the sound our feet make walking through the woods in the leaves. We laughed and tried to run in them, but we couldn't go very fast. I sometimes wish I could take my grandkids there, but the trees are all gone, houses now have been built where the trees once stood, and my grandparents are no longer living.

One year when Louise and I were both in high school, our Uncle W.A. and our Aunt Judy took us to Ohio during our Christmas break. After much discussion with mom, she decided to let us go with them for a week. The trip was one I will always remember. We had never gone to any of their homes and we got to visit a day with each of them. I still remember Judy had made a carrot cake. I remember Aunt Faye had made a gelatin dessert with fruit and nuts in it, Aunt Gloria made Apple Crisp using dry cake mix and butter, and we ended our day with Uncle Oscar and Aunt Doris taking us to see the Eden Park Holiday display and a toy train display at a home in Ohio.

One of our days we spent with our cousins, Jim, Jr., Sharon, and Brenda Caddell. They were very musical, too. They had a double keyboard organ with foot pedals. I remember Jr. going down on the floor and playing the pedals with his hands while I played on the keys. We did a duet of "The Beverly Hillbillies" theme song. I still remember the laughter.

I remember the weather and every detail about that week. It was special and I hold a special place in my heart for my Uncle W.A. Perkins for thinking of us and giving us this trip. He brought us back at the end of the week safe and sound.

<u>Corinthians 13:13</u>—*And now abideth faith, hope, love, these three; but the greatest of these [is] love.*

COUSINS AND OTHER KIN FOLK

Some of my best memories are of my childhood when my cousins would come to visit. We had a huge family on both sides, but we always had room for anyone that wanted to spend the night. My mom would bring quilts and pillows out for everyone. I didn't mind giving up my bed for an adult that might be staying. Sleeping on the floor was different, and I didn't seem to have any trouble sleeping when we had company.

I remember aunts and uncles visiting and just dropping in. My Uncle Orville and Aunt Gloria Perkins would usually come to see us when they came in from Ohio. I still remember Uncle Orville's hearty laugh that seemed infectious as everyone laughed with him. They had no children so we came to expect that we would see them often as Christmas and Easter holidays would give way to time for celebration. Even as we got older, married, and came back to have a holiday meal at mom and dad's, they would find a way to get there if they felt like it. We looked forward to seeing them.

We saw mom's sister, Aunt Faye and Uncle Walter Caddell, and their children, Jr., Sharon, and Brenda usually visited during the summer. We would enjoy hanging out with them, and mom would usually cook some hearty meals for the family. We were more concerned with playing than eating. They were about the same age as my sister and brother, so we had a lot in common. They lived in Ohio, and we had plenty of acres to explore and it was always an adventure.

In the Summer, when the school had ended for that year, Uncle Harold, and Aunt Morna West would bring Joan, June, Ruth Ann, and Ledford to our house and let them stay for a month. We loved it. We had extra people to help with our chores of breaking up beans and gathering wood to keep the fire going when mom canned outside. We also had someone to laugh with as we would constantly be playing and doing things to play pranks on each other. My mom treated them just the same as she did her own children. "Her house, her rules" was pretty much how it was going to be. If one of the cousins was causing a problem, she punished them the same as she did her own. We respected them and they respected us.

I remember one Summer when Ledford, one of the cousins, came to see us; he had a pony. Of course, everyone wanted to ride the pony. I tried to get on it, but I couldn't get the hang of it. I kept falling off, but the exhausted pony probably wanted to die after we all took turns trying to ride this little animal, with no saddle. That creature didn't stay very long. Summer was soon over, and the pony must have left with it.

<u>Proverbs 22:6</u>—*Train up a child in the way he should go: and when he is old, he will not depart from it.*

IMAGINATION STATION

When I was young, I pretended I could be a homemaker, baking mud cakes and pies when I was just a little girl. We had a wooded area across the road from our house, where we had a hog lot that usually sheltered two big hogs. These were being fattened for taking to the slaughterhouse in the fall for putting in the freezer. We could play in that area outside of the pig lot because we didn't have to fear snakes as it had been said that pigs would kill snakes. We would dig up small trees and gather rocks. After we had gathered enough, we would align the border of our area we intended to use for our playhouse with the rocks and plant small trees, as if we had landscaped our yard. Much to my amazement, the small trees were still there many years later, only much taller.

We didn't have any toy dishes, so we used canning lids and any small container, such as a coffee can, to pretend we had a furnished kitchen. Trees and rocks were our toys. There was no cost involved and it kept us busy. In those days, we didn't have to fear that there might be mean people lurking around waiting to grab one of us and take us away. For one thing, we never played alone. We always had our brothers and sisters with us, as well as any cousins that might be visiting. We also had been told by my dad, many times, "I don't want you starting fights, but, by jacks, you better take your part if someone starts to fight with you." I am pretty sure the whole neighborhood was safer because of those wise words.

Genesis 11:6—*And the LORD said, Behold, the people [is] one, and they have all one language; and this they begin to do: and now nothing will be restrained from them, which they have imagined to do.*

NO SHOES, NO POLISH, NO PROBLEM

In the Summer, we hardly ever wore shoes, except on Sunday, when we played in the yard. Mom had a unique way of having my sister Louise and I polish our shoes. She would buy black patent leather shoes and on Sunday morning, before church, she would give us a biscuit after breakfast. She had us rub a biscuit over the shoe to make it shiny. It really worked. It was unusual and we always had biscuits leftover from breakfast. One biscuit would take care of both pairs of shoes and be very cost effective. I can imagine, if dogs started licking our shoes it was because they smelled the aroma of the biscuit lingering on the leather.

Going barefoot did have its disadvantages. Bees like the clover and the clover is so soft to walk upon until you meet the bees. Stings hurt, but a variety of things can ease the pain and swelling. First, and foremost, snake oil could be rubbed on the affected area. This was my Grandpa West's favorite remedy. Second, turpentine could be used. Both of these methods have lingering smells that are very unpleasant, but it could have taken our mind off the pain we were feeling from the sting. I have heard that chewing tobacco can be chewed and moistened tobacco can be applied to the area, but I never tried it because nobody used tobacco at my house and we were only interested in multi-purpose remedies. If chewing tobacco had ever been brought into our house, I might have taken that habit up, but it wasn't ever there so it was never a problem.

Samuel 15:30—*And David went up by the ascent of mount Olivet, and wept as he went up, and had his head covered, and he went barefoot: and all the people that was with him covered every man his head, and they went up, weeping as they went up.*

CHOOSE YOUR BATTLES

When mom came home from having my brother Roger, my Grandpa West and Uncle Charles came by to visit and Roger, being a newborn baby, was all red and wrinkly. Grandpa said, "I believe he is an Indian; he's so red." Grandpa knew I would argue with him, and he was only saying this to get my temper flared up. I should have been a lawyer as I liked to argue and today was no different. I was only getting close to six, but I argued with him, and I still remember Grandpa laughing about it.

He loved to play pranks, too. I don't ever remember hearing him call me by my name. He always referred to me as "Girl". He would refer to my Grandma West as "Woman" often, especially when he wanted to watch wrestling on television, and she wanted to watch Porter Wagner and Dolly Parton. He would say, "Woman, let me watch this show and you can watch the television after wrestling goes off". Grandma would give in and not argue, but she would start singing something like "Amazing Grace" and Grandpa would just try to ignore her.

Since there was only one television set in the home and only two channels would come in on the set, Grandma had no other choice but to practice her singing while Grandpa continued to offer his mighty jabs of right, then left, and right again as he got into the wrestling as if he was right in the ring with the wrestlers.

<u>Ephesians 6:12</u>—*For we wrestle not against flesh and blood, but against principalities, against powers, against the rulers of the darkness of this world, against spiritual wickedness in high places.*

HAIRDOS I WILL NEVER FORGET

I remember how my mom would do my hair when I was about three and I hated it. She took a small amount of hair right on top of my head and made a 'pin-curl' out of it. I absolutely did not like it. We were living in a basement apartment in Michigan. One evening, we had company over, and I had gone into the bedroom to play while the adults visited. I saw my mom's scissors lying on the dresser where she had been mending some clothes. I looked at the scissors and suddenly felt powerful enough to change my life. I was afraid, but fear wasn't as strong as the urge for a change. I cut the 'pin-curl' off at the scalp with those sewing scissors. I stayed in the bedroom until the people left. When they left, my mom came into my bedroom to check on me. She screamed and yelled at me, then spanked me, but I never had that 'pin-curl' again. I don't remember anything she said, but I do remember the loud yelling and then it became worse as she tried to pull more hair up to hide the obvious spot. If there had been a clothesline and she picked me up and pinned me on it, it could not have hurt any worse. I had to have even more hideous hairdos for a while until the hair grew back on top of my head. I knew my career as a beautician was short lived.

When I was about six, "Spoolies" were the latest craze. The little flexible, rubber contraption allowed one to wind hair around the center and fold the top over to hold the "Spoolie" in place. I could wind my own hair on the "Spoolie" and sleep in them with no trouble. In the morning, all I had to do was open the "Spoolie" and unwind the lock of hair. Those were easy for a six-year-old to manipulate and it was really "hands-on" learning. I was definitely a "Spoolie Doolie" girl. My mom always did the haircuts for me. I always had the cowlick to deal with on the right side of my face and a round face that always ended up looking like a bowl had been placed on my head to make the hairdo.

When I was in fifth grade my mother decided to give me a home perm. If a perm gave lots of curls, it was referred to as "it took". It "took" all right. My hair was frizzed and kinky curly. I decided to just wear a scarf over my hair at school. The teacher made me remove the scarf in the classroom.

Roaring laughter was all I remember when I removed the scarf. The Bozo look was not popular then. I didn't like the response from the classroom and decided that very day I would never let my mom do that to me again. I never had another perm until I was about 40. Then, it was not a frizzy perm, but a body perm and I let a professional do it. I remember when my brother Jerry was about two. My Uncle Fred Smith had some hair clippers. He would pin clothespins on Jerry's ears and have him crying and then Fred would laugh as he proceeded to give him his "special" for the day. Later, mom got some of those clippers and she cut hair for my three brothers and my dad. Sometimes the cuts were good and sometimes there were white spots on the side of their heads where she made a mistake or maybe she was trying to learn to carve like the chainsaw artists; close call there. After a few days or weeks, the difference in a good haircut and a bad haircut was about a month.

When the boys were in high school, the trend was for boys to have their hair grown out and to have sideburns. Mom would set up shop in the kitchen. She didn't go to school for this, but she could do about any other thing she wanted to do, why not cut hair? She had barber scissors, a comb, and some really sharp clippers. My mom trimmed their hair, and when it was time for Jerry, he told her he wanted her to just trim it and let it be a little longer than usual. Dad was not in the room while the hair cutting was taking place. He was sitting in the living room watching the news. Jerry and dad met somewhere in the light a few minutes after the haircut and dad made mom give him another one. He made reference to asking if Jerry was wanting to grow it out long enough to see through it. Of course, Jerry got another haircut—not the one he wanted, but it would be the one dad wanted him to have.

My brother Roger told me of a time when mom accidentally shaved one of his eyebrows off while she was supposed to give him a haircut. I am sure Roger had to comb his hair differently for a few days, at least, or, he may have just shaved the other side to match. He might have just started a new style and didn't let anyone know so it didn't catch on, as I recall. Knowing Roger, he may have gotten sympathy from his teacher and made her think his hair was mysteriously falling out.

Matthew 10:30—*But the very hairs of your head are all numbered.*

HELP BUT DO NOT HINDER

We were taught to not get in the way and to be helpful to anyone that needed help. I vividly remember when mom went to the clinic, in Williamsburg, to have my brother Roger, I was almost six years old. It was hot and he was born on the 4th of July. Aunt Genny, one of my mom's younger sisters, came over to help with us children when mom went into labor.

My mom had given strict orders and told me to help Aunt Genny any way she needed help. As I recall, Aunt Genny started to make some biscuits and had her bread pans ready, oven pre-heated, and she turned her back for a minute to get something and I stuck my hand down in the biscuit dough to 'help her make biscuits'. I had not started to school, about five years old, couldn't follow a recipe, and didn't know I would only get in trouble for this. Aunt Genny turned around, and the next thing I know, she swatted my bottom and told me that she didn't need my help. I was so confused. I kept thinking to myself, "What was that all about? I was only trying to help!"

I just stepped back and walked away to go back into the room where the new baby was and waited for my next assignment of duty, whatever that might have been.

<u>Proverbs 3:5-6</u> —*Trust in the LORD with all thine heart; and lean not unto thine own understanding.*

WRESTLING WITH A BEAST IN THE WASHING MACHINE

Before I went to school, dad was working away from home in Lexington, Kentucky. He would "batch" during the week and come home on the weekend. Mom would wash his clothes and get things done during the week so he would have clean clothes to take back to Lexington for the next week.

One particular day in the summer, she had opened the window in the room where her wringer washer was situated. There was no screen on the window. Bees were flying around outside, and the sun quickly dried any sheets or towels hung on the clothesline. She had washed clothes all day and we had been in and out the back door several times playing and going with her to the outside clothesline. After she had finished washing all of the clothes, she had to drain the washer.

As the last couple of inches of water were coming out of the washing machine, into the bucket to be poured outside, my mom noticed something wiggle in the water. It was a very long black snake! They are harmless if one bites you, but fear of snakes might cause one to have a heart attack. My mom, the quick thinker, went to the backyard and got a garden hoe and dug the snake out of the washer and managed to get it out with the hoe and carry it outside without dropping it. I still remember the snake wiggling and how she carefully kept it on the end of the hoe. As soon as she got it outside, the hoe became the weapon of death for the snake.

1 Peter 4:12—*Beloved, think it not strange concerning the fiery trial, which is to try you, as though some strange thing happened unto you:*

FOODS I NEVER WANT TO EAT AGAIN

There are a few foods that I have tried to eat, but I hope I never have to eat again. I remember my Aunt Ora bringing potato salad to our house one Sunday afternoon. I had never eaten olives as my mother insisted, we didn't like them, so she never bought them. The potato salad was covered with sliced olives and was so pretty. I really didn't know what they were, so I got a generous helping on my plate. My mom was right after all; I did not like olives. I still remember that peculiar taste that seemed to linger on and on. I tried pushing the potato salad around with my fork, but it was obvious that I had wasted that food.

Aunt Ora also brought some Limburger cheese. I remember it was all wrapped up neatly in a piece of freezer paper and it had been purchased at the local grocery store. I had never seen, nor smelled, this kind of cheese before. I still remember the odor, not smell, just plain old odor, from this brown paper bag. It resembled the smell of dirty tennis shoes to me. The day was hot and even though the windows were open in the house, the smell was horrible.

I can eat salmon, tuna, shrimp, and really fresh catfish if it is cooked properly. I do not like the taste of seafood salad, crab meat, frog legs, or undercooked fish of any kind. Having tried all of the ones I just mentioned has caused me to have a fear of ever tasting Sushi. I have eaten alligator, and as many things have been described, "It tastes like chicken"; I only thought the batter that had been deeply fried resembled fried chicken, but only in a fried chicken kind of way.

My Grandma West used to take fresh green peas, make some type of dumpling dough, and make what she called "Pea Dumplings". This slimy green mess was the worst looking dish I ever saw her make when I was a child. I never even tried them, but even now while I think about it, I still don't want to know how they tasted. She cooked the peas. She then proceeded to drop the dumpling dough into the boiling, green peas kettle, boiled until the dumplings were done, and the rest is history. My mom used to make a frosting for cakes that she called "Minute Icing". She took a cup of sugar, two tablespoons of cocoa, two tablespoons of butter, a teaspoon of vanilla, and one-fourth cup of milk. She would mix it all together and when it started to boil, she would recite the Lord's prayer. By the time she finished reciting the prayer, the frosting was ready. One evening, she had made supper and a cake for dessert. She made the frosting, but she hadn't tasted it before it went on the cake. Dad was the first to be served this cake. The first bite he took made him push his plate away. She mistakenly used a cup of salt instead of a cup of sugar. It did change the quality of the dessert. She was not impressed with our laughter. Maybe she should have read **Isaiah 53:4**. *"He took our suffering on him and felt our pain for us,"* after she realized what she had done.

Genesis 9:3—*Every moving thing that liveth shall be meat for you; even as the green herb have, I given you all things.*

THE CRACKER JACK SURPRISE

I had many relatives who lived in Ohio. My Aunt Marie and Uncle Tom lived in Fairborn, Ohio and came in to visit my grandparents one weekend. My cousin Kathy, their daughter, wanted to know if I could ride to Williamsburg with them as they needed to take grandma to get some groceries. When my grandmother smiled at me as I got into the car, I wanted to laugh, but I tried to hold back. They had brought snacks with them, and grandma had been offered a box of cracker jacks. She had bit down on a hard peanut and broke one of her front false teeth out. She couldn't get it fixed as no dentist was available on Saturday. She would have to look this way all weekend. Every time she would speak, or smile, my cousin and I would try not to laugh but the harder we tried not to laugh, the worse it became for us. Grandma finally said, "I just don't see what you think is so funny!" That just made it worse. I tried hiding my face into my sleeve and my cousin was laughing, too, so I couldn't stop. My stomach was sore from laughing so hard.

While we were trying to settle down, my Uncle Tom told us about when he was growing up. He had a brother that was mentally challenged. He and his friends decided to go to the Lane Theater and watch a movie. They all bought Cracker Jacks for their snack before the movie. They watched the movie and when they came outside, they started asking each other what they had gotten as their prize in the boxes of Cracker Jacks. His brother said, "I don't know what I got. I ate mine." This made us laugh again and when grandma looked at us laughing, we saw her missing tooth and laughed even harder. Why do we laugh at other's misery? We all do this at some time or other.

Proverbs 17:22—*A merry heart doeth good [like] a medicine: but a broken spirit drieth the bones.*

CLEANING UP WHEN YOU DON'T HAVE A BATHROOM IN THE HOUSE

We had a large washtub that mom used when she washed our clothes in the wringer washer. The wash tub held the water that she would use to rinse our clothes before she fed them through the wringer and hang them outside on the clothesline on warm, breezy days. When we had to take a bath, the washtub was used for that, too. We had an outhouse that was used for other personal things you always do in bathrooms. You don't have to worry about plumbing issues when you have an outhouse.

At night, we would try to remember to not drink anything late, go to the little 8 lb. metal lard bucket in the kitchen closet to prevent having to go to the outhouse, and place our clothes where we could find them as we could wear them the second day if they hadn't gotten dirty during the day. I think I was about 12 when we got the bathroom installed. Now, I don't think about that much, but am thankful for the bathrooms, even if I do take them for granted.

Grandma West always referred to her pot as a chamber pot. Some people refer to them as thunder pots. She would empty hers before she went to bed. One night, she proceeded to take the pot to the back door and throw it out and someone was prowling around her house. She threw the contents of the pot on the "would-be" intruder. Without a doubt, the chamber pot prevented someone from going to prison. Maybe the intruder would have preferred to go to prison.

Isaiah 1:16 *Wash you, make you clean; put away the evil of your doings from before mine eyes; cease to do evil.*

THE NEED FOR MORE THAN A PATH

Being the third child in this family, I remember some of the life at our house before major plumbing. My parents missed being close to their parents and wanted to get back closer to their home. Dad and mom built a modest house consisting of a living room, kitchen, dining room, three bedrooms and a "path". They didn't live there very long before they went to Michigan, but it was all paid for, as dad never bought anything on credit.

I remember after moving to Michigan and back to Kentucky, then back to Michigan and again back to Kentucky, our family had grown and there was a great need for a bathroom in the house. We also needed more bedroom space to accommodate the three boys. A bedroom was built upstairs for the boys. Two full size beds were placed upstairs, and a closet was built.

I still remember the day we got the bathroom ready to use. It was a wonderful day. We probably wore the commode flushing device out those first few days just trying it out. It was a highlight of that year. It was a great alternative to what had been our lifestyle.

Philippians 4:19—*But my God shall supply all your need according to his riches in glory by Christ Jesus.*

NEEDING NEW SHOES

*I*t is a fact of life, that children outgrow shoes very fast. Sometimes, children have bigger feet than their parents and they are only in the fifth grade. When there is only one store that carries a variety of shoes among other essentials, your choices are often limited. If we needed a new pair of shoes, especially for school, mom would have us go out and get a small limb from one of the trees and she would measure the length of our foot and then put the limb in her purse and she would use the limb to determine which shoes she would purchase for us. She didn't have to get shoes for everyone at the same time, so we never got the limbs mixed up.

She would stick the limb into the shoe she was considering determining if there was enough "wiggle room" for our toes. Sometimes, we got saddle oxfords; sometimes we got penny loafers, and sometimes we got just plain old slip-on shoes that were not very stylish, but they served a purpose. Louise and I wore the same size shoes when we were in high school, so we switched out with each other, giving us twice the options. Having an older sister sometimes had many advantages. I was able to have more choices for my wardrobe.

Exodus 3:5: *And he said, Draw not nigh hither: put off thy shoes from off thy feet, for the place whereon thou standest [is] holy ground.*

CATCHING CHICKENS

When I was growing up, my Grandpa West raised chickens commercially. He had two big houses full of baby chicks that changed each week as the chickens grew into fryers. When the chicks are little, they look like a river of yellow flowing in the floor of the houses because all you can see is the yellow fluff. As they grow into fryers, they turn from yellow to white and it looks like a dust storm when they are scurrying to get out of the way of the caretaker. The smell is horrible, and I cannot describe it but I can smell it in my mind now as I write.

When the chickens are fully grown, catching chickens to load on the trucks was a community effort. Even before we had landline phones, my uncle and grandpa would ride in the truck and let the neighbors know we were having a 'chicken-catching' on a certain date. The whole family would go. The semi-truck, loaded with crates would be parked near the chicken houses and about 7:00 PM the men and children, old enough to work and carry up to eight chickens at a time, would work in the chicken house and carry the chickens to the truck drivers and hand them up. My cousins would team up with my sister and me because we couldn't carry eight chickens each. We would race to see who could carry the most chickens. This was a smelly, hard-to-breathe, kind of game that never awarded a grand prize.

While this was going on, the women were busy making Kool-Aid to drink and bologna sandwiches for the workers to enjoy after the task was finished. We would wash our hands at the outside spigot and sit on the porch and steps of my grandparents' house.

As the last cages were filled with chickens, the big truck would be heard going past our house later that night. Squawking chickens sound pretty loud when there are several hundred of them on a truck. One of us would hear the truck coming down the road and would yell for the brothers and sisters. We would all sit on the porch and watch. We would listen for the truck, as our house was on a dirt road and very few trucks ever came on our road unless it might be a coal truck bringing winter coal for heating. I never thought much about those chickens except that they had no idea what they were heading for no more than I did. The chickens had no way of knowing that the squawking they made as they traveled that dirt road would be the last communication they would have with their buddies on this earth. Like the chickens, we don't know when our last day may be, so we need to be ready to go when our appointed time to die comes.

Matthew 23:37—*O Jerusalem, Jerusalem, [thou] that killest the prophets, and stonest them which are sent unto thee, how often would I have gathered thy children together, even as a hen gathereth her chickens under [her] wings, and ye would not!*

GRANDMA AND THE BISCUIT EATING NEIGHBOR

We sometimes would visit Grandma and Grandpa West and get to spend the night with them. My grandmother made heavy quilts. These quilts hurt our feet; they were so heavy, but she wanted to make sure we were warm. They heated the little house with two fireplaces that were back-to-back. One was in the living room, and one was in the bedroom. She cooked on a cast iron coal cook stove. She had to have wood for the stove and kindling to start the fire. Her kitchen was very tiny, but she raised her family in that house. I still have that stove. I bought it from my grandmother when she was staying with my mom and dad. The stove is a great reminder of them.

One particular Saturday evening, I was staying with my grandma while grandpa fed the chickens. She had been cooking supper and had it on the stove warming while we waited for grandpa to get back into the house. We heard the door open, and grandma thought it was grandpa coming in from feeding the chickens. She said, "Russ, Is that you?"

He didn't answer so she got up, and as she got to the doorway, she saw what was in the kitchen, and she grabbed the side of the wall almost fainting. She could hardly say anything because she was so startled. It was not grandpa; it was the neighbor's coon dog. It was just finishing off the last biscuit grandma had baked. Grandma was so scared she couldn't speak. We managed to get the dog back outside and grandma had to start cooking supper all over again. She was a very clean woman and never had animals in the house.

Maybe the dog had a bath before it came inside. We didn't know. We just assumed it had not and proceeded to start over.

A few minutes later, when grandpa came in, grandma told him what had happened. His comment to her was, "Well, at least your cooking was fit for a dog to eat." She didn't laugh as hard as he did. I wish I could have taken a picture of that event.

Psalm 22:20— *Deliver my soul from the sword; my darling from the power of the dog.*

CHARLES' TALE ABOUT CHRISTMAS GIFTS

Dad's brother, Charles West, told me about my dad and his sister Delores buying Christmas gifts for the whole family when they started working and earning their own money. They decided that since both of them were now earning money, they would buy gifts for everyone in the home. They never had Christmas gifts and thought it would be a special surprise for the family. They ordered toys and other things from a mail-order catalog. The things had to be picked up at the post office near their home on Alsile Road.

The packages came in and Charles and his brothers went to the post office and picked them up. Instead of leaving them in the wrapper, Charles decided to look into the package he was supposed to receive. It was a toy truck filled with hard candy. That candy smelled so good and sweet and looked so tempting. Charles decided to get a piece or two before he went outside to gather firewood, one that would never be missed. He put a few pieces in his pocket. He ate it while he did his evening chores.

The next evening, he put a few more pieces in his pocket and enjoyed the candy while he worked outside doing his routine chores. On Christmas day, everyone was sitting around the living room anxiously awaiting opening the gifts because they never had money to splurge and buy Christmas gifts before, and Delores and my dad felt honored to make this year special for each of them. When Charles opened his gift, the toy truck did not have any candy in it because Charles had eaten it all a piece or two at a time until it was all gone. My dad was furious and said, "By jacks, if you are going to be that way, I will never buy you another Christmas gift." I can almost hear my dad saying that. Knowing that any time I heard dad say, "By jacks" in a sentence, he was getting angry. I can almost hear Uncle Charles' laughter as he told the story to me.

Corinthians 12:4-11 *4Now there are diversities of gifts, but the same Spirit. 5And there are differences of administrations, but the same LORD. 6And there are diversities of operations, but it is the same God which worketh all in all. 7But the manifestation of the Spirit is given to every man to profit withal. 8For to one is given by the Spirit the word of wisdom; to another the word of knowledge by the same Spirit; 9To another faith by the same Spirit; to another the gifts of healing by the same Spirit; 10To another the working of miracles; to another prophecy; to another discerning of spirits; to another divers kinds of tongues; to another the interpretation of tongues: 11But all these worketh that one and the selfsame Spirit, dividing to every man severally as he will.*

HALLOWEEN AND NOT TRICK OR TREATING

I remember the way Halloween was regarded at our house. "Begging" was how our dad looked at it. I remember mom making my costume for school in first grade. I took it to school and even wore it, but I was afraid of all the scary people and cried until I got to go home. I remember that evening our family went to Williamsburg and dad drove us through town to see all the people dressed in their costumes walking from door to door in the town. That was when Williamsburg had businesses and two-way traffic. We never went to anyone's house on Halloween. We stayed home and nobody came to our house, either. I remember one Halloween, our Uncle Vess Ball, and Aunt Nettie dressed up in some old clothes and came to our house and brought candy and fruit to us. I'll never forget them for that and for always trying to make us feel good about our circumstances. They always had a smile for everyone. They somehow knew that we never went to get candy like the other people in our community and just brought it to us. Our Aunt Delores, dad's sister, had three boys and she always let her boys go trick or treating. She talked dad into letting us go with them. I still remember dad complaining in the car as he drove from house to house letting us "beg", as he referred to it. I remember when we got home, mom made us put all the candy together and she would ration it out to us when she wanted. No cavities for us! That was the first and last time we had any fun going trick-or-treating.

Proverbs 22:6—*Train up a child in the way he should go: and when he is old, he will not depart from it.*

LOOKING FOR A CHRISTMAS TREE

Even when it looked like Christmas was going to be a holiday with no money for gifts, we always put up a tree. One particular year, mom didn't feel like going out to look for one, but she told us how she wanted the tree to look. She insisted that pine would be better than cedar or spruce. Louise, Jerry, and I went to the woods with a small hatchet to find the best pine tree we could find. We couldn't find any that were perfect, but we managed to find two trees that were about six feet tall.

We took the trees home, each of us thinking that only one tree would be considered the best. When we got there, mom decided that it would take both of those trees together to make a Christmas tree that was not too lop-sided. The tree was still awful looking, and it wouldn't stand up straight. We decorated with lots of silver rope and ice cycles. It would try to tip over, but we had hoped it would make it through the Christmas holiday.

On Christmas morning, I was up early. Mom was already in the kitchen making breakfast. Bacon was frying and biscuits were already in the oven. I managed to ease out of the kitchen and go into the living room to look at the tree somehow hoping it had some magic added to it and it would look better. That didn't happen. I got too close to the tree, and "boom" down came the tree. Water from the bottom of the tree and all came pouring right on all of the packages. It made a huge mess. Mom decided I knocked it over, but I promise, I didn't do it. The tree just fell over. I still got a spanking for being near the tree and mom thinking I got too close to it. I decided next Christmas I will just sleep in.

Jeremiah 10:6 *For the customs of the people are vain: for one cutteth a tree out of the forest, the work of the hands of the workman, with the axe. 4They deck it with silver and with gold; they fasten it with nails and with hammers, that it move not. 5They are upright as the palm tree, but speak not: they must needs be borne, because they cannot go. Be not afraid of them; for they cannot do evil, neither also is it in them to do good. 6Forasmuch as there is none like unto thee, O LORD; thou art great, and thy name is great in might.*

PICKING BLACKBERRIES

In July, usually around July 4th, we gathered our buckets and put on old clothes and boots and headed out to the blackberry patch. We usually would start early in the morning as it would be very hot up in the day. We would take Trixie, our dog, with us to make sure there were no copperhead snakes wanting to take a bite out of us. Trixie was faithful to her job. She would bark and mom would take a hoe and kill the copperhead, or other snake, if she could get to it.

One particular day, Trixie got into a struggle with a copperhead and got bitten on the head. Her head was swollen to double its size. Mom took kerosene and coated the dog's head in this, and the dog got better and lived. It was miserable for a few days, but this remedy saved the dog's life. Blackberries are sticky and gnats bother you when you are trying to pick berries. It would be worth the work when we got home for lunch. We would usually have at least two or three gallons of blackberries. Mom would take a portion of the berries and make some blackberry syrup for us to enjoy on some big fluffy homemade pancakes. I can still remember the smell of the pancakes and especially the syrup. It might have been because we were so hungry from being outside picking berries all morning, but that seemed so delicious to us.

One year, the boys picked blackberries and took to Campbell's Store, on HWY 92. I asked Ralph, my brother, what they received for their efforts, and he said that he remembered getting a spanking because his friend, Paul, told him to fill the bottom of the bucket with rocks and put black berries on top and they would get more money. I think they got $1 a gallon for those berries. The plot to fool the buyers failed but Ralph remembered that lesson well. As I have stated before, lessons learned the hard way will stick with you. I am sure Ralph thought of that day many times when he saw blackberries ready for the picking.

Isaiah 7:24 *Men will come there with bows and arrows, because all the land will be full of blackberries and thorns.*

PAGEANTS

I remember when I was a senior in high school I was told, because of my grades, I was eligible to participate in the "Miss Whitley County High School" Pageant. We were given the guidelines, and I went home and asked my mom about it. Of course, I got to wear my sister's prom dress. It was too big for me, so we used pins to make it work. This was the first time I had ever been to a beauty shop in my life. I usually trimmed my own hair, always, so this was a very new experience for me. We didn't have to do anything special, such as talent, as it was voted upon by the faculty of the high school. We got matched up with the guys that also had good grades. One guy that no girl had matched up with asked if he could be my escort. He was scared, too. I will not put his real name in this book as he has since changed his name. I didn't win, but it was a good, competitive activity that made me feel good about myself.

After high school, I attended Cumberland College. I remember in my junior year, one of my professor's nephews was visiting and he came to college quite often with her. He enrolled and we became good friends. Nominations were being taken for the "Miss Cumberland College" pageant. This pageant required a formal gown, a bathing suit, and a talent to participate. Steve nominated me. I received word that I had been nominated and I was excited to go home and tell my mom. She wasn't as excited as I was about the event. I told her I would make my gown. At that time, being extremely skinny, I could wear children's clothes. I couldn't go anywhere to buy anything. I had to shop for a bathing suit, so I went into the Youthland Fashions Store on Main Street, in

Williamsburg, at that time. I found a bathing suit there. It had to be one piece and a solid color. The only solid color bathing suit they had that fit me was purple. I bought it. I then had to concentrate on the talent. If we sang, we couldn't have anyone except the college band play for us. I went to the Music Shop on Main street and bought a "Carpenter's Album" and intended on meeting with the band director to arrange for music. I never got that far into the process as my mom complained about everything I was having to purchase, even though I made my own money from selling Avon in my spare time. Every day, I would come home exhausted from school and had to hear the complaints. One night, I wrote a nice letter to Ms. Sue Weedman explaining that I was dropping out of the pageant due to the fact that I could not make time for it now. The truth was, I just didn't think I could continue with this yelling every day. I took the letter to the office where she worked and left it. I never heard from Ms. Weedman anymore. I didn't even tell my mother what I was going to do until I had already taken the letter. She never said anything about the situation when I told her what I had done. She never even gave me a second glance of regret. She just kept peeling potatoes for supper. When my friend Steve, found out what I had done, he was upset but he didn't understand what was going on. I couldn't dare explain it as I was embarrassed.

When our eldest daughter was in Kindergarten, the school had a pageant that included one representative from each grade. Clarissa was selected to represent Kindergarten. We collected change and the penny votes were allowed right up until the last minute before the winner was announced. The event was a school Fall Festival. During the last five minutes, the money started to be accepted by checks. One man got upset because our daughter was winning. He looked at my father-in- law and shouted as the winner was announced, "Big preacher with a pocketbook, that is how she won!" I never let the girls be in any more pageants that revolved around money being collected. It was not fair to the children and every parent sees their child as the winner.

Angelina was in a pageant when she was in grade school. She represented Wofford Elementary School. We went to Somerset to a Bridal Shop and bought her a dress. She had long blond hair and looked very beautiful as she marched out onto the same floor where I had been when I was in the high school pageant. She won in her category. Another girl cried and cried because her parents had spent $500 on her dress, and she didn't win. What can we learn from pageants? The same thing we see in everyday life. There's always going to be somebody that wants what you have, tries to keep you from enjoying yourself and will go to great lengths to make sure you cannot succeed. Not much more than that can be learned, from my perspective. These lessons are the hardest ones to learn, but they stay with you.

<u>Timothy 2:9-10</u> *In like manner also, that women adorn themselves in modest apparel, with shamefacedness and sobriety; not with broided hair, or gold, or pearls, or costly array; But (which becometh women professing godliness) with good works.*

GATHER NO DUST

My grandma was a devoted wife and mother. She would always lay grandpa's clothes out that he would wear after he shaved and got ready to go to town. One particular day, I was taken to Grandma's to stay with her while my mom took Grandpa to town. He was ready when mom brought me there. Grandma was busy dusting the furniture in the bedroom. We had been busy cleaning up her house and I heard her yell out, "Oh my Lord !!!"

I thought something had happened. I hurriedly went to see what was wrong. She informed me that she had made a big mistake. She had a can of lemon furniture polish on the bed instead of his deodorant can. He had used it and never even knew it happened. My grandpa was blind in one eye due to an accident he had in the mines. She was worried, so I said to her, "Well, at least he won't gather any dust today". We both laughed but I am not sure what she told Grandpa West. If that had been me, I would never have said anything, but I am sure grandma told him about it. She always wanted the best for him.

<u>Ecclesiastes 12:7</u>—*Then shall the dust return to the earth as it was: and the spirit shall return unto God who gave it.*

MOVING UP THE CHICKEN CHAIN

Mom would make a fried chicken meal for our whole family of two adults and seven children with one chicken. She was not going to waste any part of the chicken. She cut the chicken into sections like this. There were two chicken breasts, one "pulley" bone, two thighs, two legs, two wings, and the back, heart and gizzard were stewed for another meal.

The order the chicken pieces were dispensed as follows: Dad and mom each got a chicken breast; Louise got a pulley bone; Carolyn and Jerry each got a thigh; Ralph and Roger each got a leg, and Diane and Pam got to chew on the wings and neck, I suppose. There was always lots of crunchy bits on the chicken and she always fried the chicken in a cast iron skillet.

I used to laugh and tell everyone that I didn't even know a chicken had white meat until Louise got married and I moved up the chicken chain. I felt like it was a special occasion the first time we had chicken after Louise left home as I got to get the most-favored white meat piece of chicken, the pulley bone. Mom told me to quit saying that, but I liked to say it, even when she wasn't around.

Romans 2:11—*For there is no respect of persons with God.*

UNFORGETTABLE FUNERALS

I remember going to the funeral of my great-grandmother, Leter Carr. It was the first funeral I recall ever attending. I was about five and it was before I went to school. I remember seeing her lying in the casket and not moving. I observed the shiny satin that lined the casket. I watched as everyone went by the casket, and nobody was saying anything to her. She just kept being still. It made me wonder why nobody was saying anything to her. They were talking beside her but not to her. Some were drying tears, and some just found a seat as they made their way past her casket. The funeral and burial were all on the same day. She is buried in the Alsile Cemetery, as are many other relatives.

They had her funeral at the Tabernacle Church in Williamsburg. I was afraid. It didn't seem like a joyous occasion and my dad's mother, my grandmother, was crying, something I rarely saw her do.

I remember going to my aunt Cora Faulkner's home and visiting with the family after the funeral. One of the children had a peddle car. I thought that was the best toy I had ever seen. I still think that. I never had one, but I sure loved playing on that one. We took turns rolling it on the sidewalk. The nearby bushes had blooms on them, and we would swipe against them as we rolled along and the air would smell like perfume.

I sometimes think of that when I smell the fragrance from flowers or bushes. It's funny how our memories are jogged by a simple breeze and a flower garden. I have always loved having fragrant flowers in my yard. The fragrance of roses' perfume reminds me of funerals. Roses are not my favorite flowers because of that very thing. I prefer lilies and wildflowers, especially daisies.

When my Grandma West passed away, she was buried on, May 12, the day after her birthday. While we were at the cemetery, my niece Shaina, about six, I think at the time, managed to stand near one of the older tombstones, where she would be away from the crowd. Just before the burial, she screamed. The rustic old tombstone had fallen on her leg!

My brother Ralph grabbed her up and ran through the cemetery to take her to the doctor. Her leg was broken. We were concerned for her and prayed that Ralph would not have a car accident on the way. The travel time was probably 35 or 45 minutes on a normal day. I am sure he made the trip in about half that time. Shaina had to wear a cast for a long time. After the cast was removed, it was hard for her to walk because the cast had been so heavy. I'm sure that memory is still with Shaina, who now has three children of her own.

John 11:25—*Jesus said unto her, I am the resurrection, and the life: he that believeth in me, though he were dead, yet shall he live:*

Alsile Church

GOING TO THE DOGS

We never got to have too many pets because they weren't considered as important as the people we had living at our house. Mom never lets us have our pets on the porch or in the house. She thought animals in the house were not clean. We could sit on the porch steps with the dog but not on the porch. We had the same rules for cats. The cat would stay at the barn. If we petted the dog, mom insisted we must wash our hands immediately.

I remember a dog we had named Trixie. Trixie was a dog that had wandered to my family home from nowhere, as it probably was told: "Get out of the car; this is where you can stay because they have lots of kids." She always went with us when we had to go blackberry picking. One day, she met up with a copperhead snake and we thought she was going to die. My mom cared for her wounds by soaking a rag in kerosene and binding Trixie's head with the rag. Her head was swollen for several days, and she barely moved around. Her head resembled a basketball. She managed to get better and bounced back very quickly. Trixie was a little, mixed breed, black dog that loved to play games such as hide and seek with us. She would look under the car and see us on the other side of the car and come running to us. She never had any puppies because my mom would put her up in a safe building outside, away from the other neighborhood dogs, until it was safe to let her out. She was never neutered. She was a good dog. She never bothered with anything. One day she was crossing the road, my uncle didn't see her and ran over her. We were sad and my brothers had to bury her.

I remember having two Beagle pups before I ever went to school. Jeff and Julie were their names. Dad sold them to someone, and I never even knew he was going to sell them. I wish he had never let me even pet them if I wasn't going to get to keep them. They were only there for a little bit of time. I still remember how wiggly they both were and how it was hard to hold them because of this.

We had cattle on our farm. We had one calf we considered a pet. We had named him Elmer, like the calf showing on the glue bottle. We patted his head when we fed him in the evening. He would just stand there and lick our hands and roll his big eyes at us as he watched us on the other side of the fence. We didn't know that we would be so attached to Elmer until it came late Autumn. Dad and mom decided that Elmer was big enough to take to the slaughterhouse and packaged it into beef for the freezer to feed us in the Winter. None of us could eat the roast beef because we kept thinking about our connection to the animal we had for dinner.

When my brother Jerry was in high school, he had gotten very interested in the Future Farmers of America. In fact, he was an officer. Along with that enthusiasm came opportunities to travel to Louisville and stay in a nice hotel. Jerry had been on one of the trips and his teacher, Mr. John Holbrook, brought him home after the trip. We had another dog by this time. It was a big dog that was shaggy and sort of tan and white in color. Evidently, the dog was excited to have Jerry home and proceeded to get in the back seat of the teacher's car while they were unloading Jerry's things. We had never seen this dog do anything but sit and bark. This dog had never even been in any of our own vehicles. Mom was embarrassed and kept trying to coax the animal out of the car, but this furry animal was not thinking the same way mom was. She finally got the dog out of the car and apologized for the dog's inappropriate behavior. We were laughing the whole time the ordeal was happening. This probably scared the dog.

My brother Roger had a fish aquarium. He kept it upstairs in his room. About two years after I married, I had a fish tank set up in my living room. Clarissa liked watching the fish. One day, I cleaned the tank, mopped, and waxed the floor and Clarissa was looking at the fish. I sat down and the phone rang. All of a sudden, the tank was turned over. There were fish floating on the floor, and all my hard work was in vain. I scooped up as many as I could get and called Roger. He and my mom came over and got the fish, took them to Jellico Creek and put them in his tank. I didn't want to take a risk with that anymore, so I didn't put the tank back together.

When my girls were about 2 and 4, someone gave me a Cairn Terrier. His name was Scruffy. He was a smart dog that could fetch, sit up and roll over. One morning, I started to school and Scruffy managed to get loose and chased my car. I didn't see him chasing my car and he hit his head on the drive shaft. It instantly killed him. I felt terrible. We had only had the dog for a few weeks, and I was really upset and cried about that dog. I ended up missing work that day. Clarissa was very small and kept saying, "Mommy, why did you kill our dog?" I felt awful because I had been the last one that fed the dog and had not secured his rope properly. I tried to explain this, but she was too young to understand that it was an accident and it had not been planned.

Now, after mom died, dad was given a dog, "Tequila", which was a Dalmatian. She had unending polka dots and dad allowed her to stay inside. I don't know why the animals were allowed in the house after mom died, and grandma died, and we were all grown. That dog seemed to be a good friend for dad as all of his children were grown and married and mom was no longer living. After that dog passed away, he got another dog from the local animal shelter.

It was a mixed breed dog. He named her "Lady". He even purchased a tombstone for this dog and buried the dog near his pond.

His last dog, which recently had to be taken to the veterinarian to be put to sleep, was named "Andy". That dog didn't originally belong to him. It belonged to my nieces, Jennifer, Jessica, and Stephanie, but dad allowed it special privileges, so he claimed it. Andy developed heartworms and got very sick before we had to have him put to sleep. Dad allowed that dog to stay inside, too. I sometimes think about how attached he was to the cat, "Jasper", and how his affection for those two animals seemed to be more than it had ever been for his children. More evidence of how Alzheimer's had affected his thinking. He often forgot and wanted to feed Andy every evening after supper.

<u>Matthew 7:6</u>—*Give not that which is holy unto the dogs, neither cast ye your pearls before swine, lest they trample them under their feet, and turn again and rend you.*

LEARNING TO SEW

I was thirteen when I first learned to sew. I went to a Home Economics class and was taught the different parts of the sewing machine, how to thread a sewing machine and wind a bobbin. Upon learning about the different functions of each part of the sewing machine, we were then given strict orders not to put a thread on the machine and not have a bobbin of thread on it either. We were told to try to learn to follow the lines on a piece of notebook paper, using a knee pedal to control the sewing machine. One girl in my class declared, while the teacher was not looking, that she had one of these at home and she knew how to wind the bobbin and she was going to forego the lined notebook paper and use the thread. Her thoughts were changed as she made the biggest mess on the machine you could imagine. Special treatment had to be given to the sewing machine if it would ever be useful again. Someone had to be called in to repair the machine. We all learned from her mistake.

One project we did had to have buttonholes on the project. I carefully picked out a beautiful piece of fabric and could already see how pretty this blouse was going to be when I got finished. I stitched everything just as I had been told to until the last part—the buttonholes. I mistakenly put them on the wrong side of the blouse. In order to get our grade as complete, we had to wear the project to school. My teacher was no fool; she immediately knew that I had made a mistake. I still had enough good sewing done that I got an "A" on the report card. I did not get discouraged. I kept on sewing, every chance I got!

I went on to take Home Economics every year in high school. As my final sewing project in my senior year, I made a dark olive green, double-breasted, lined Winter coat. It was beautiful. I had never had a new coat in my whole life, that I recall. I always had to wear Louise's hand-me-downs. There was nothing wrong with that and I appreciated that she had taken care of her clothes so that I could use them. I taught myself how to crochet and made a beret to match the coat. I had knitted a matching scarf in Home Economics, too. That coat went to college with me and helped see me through three years of classes.

Mark 2:21—*No man also seweth a piece of new cloth on an old garment: else the new piece that filled it up taketh away from the old, and the rent is made worse.*

DATING, PORCH LIGHTS, AND GETTING MARRIED

Dating was not something we got much help with from mom and dad. I don't recall ever seeing them kiss except one time when dad was leaving to go to Ohio to build his sister, Violet, a house. They walked beside his truck and we watched and giggled from the inside looking out the small glass panels in the front door. I never had any dates in high school. Mom made me go with my older sister when she went on a date. I hated it. Louise and H.C. would try to fix me up with people and I knew I didn't want to go along with that. My sister was in college and was dating the man she later married, and I still had to go with them everywhere. I rebelled and told my mom I didn't want to go with them. She fussed about it, but I told her I thought it was ridiculous because she should be able to trust us by now. She trusted us with going to church unless we were sick and trusted us to take care of our younger brothers and sisters. She also trusted us to help with our elderly grandparents. We always respected our parents. I think mom didn't want us to grow up. She needed us there to help with the chores.

One night, my brother Ralph got home at 10:30 PM instead of 10:00 PM and all the doors were locked, and the lights were off. He just spent the night in his truck. Nobody came out to check on him, either. I am sure he should have come home, but I couldn't understand why he wasn't checked on.

When I went to college, my freshman year, I was asked out by a boy from Henderson, KY. He wanted to take me to some event at the college. Mom said yes only because Louise would be at that event. I was so nervous. After the date, he brought me home. My heart started to pound because I knew he was going to kiss me, and I had never been kissed. I never really went out with him again. I didn't like his laughter. He was on the Judo team at Cumberland. We would see each other at college but there was never another date with him. I then dated a couple of other guys. One was a preacher and the other wanted to date lots of girls at the same time. I later dated a guy from Barbourville. He met me in line at the sweetheart banquet that my sister and her date were going to. They knew him and he started a conversation with me while we were in line. He didn't have a car so I had to take him to my house for supper and then take him back to the dorm before my parents would allow me to go out with him. The next event that year was the SNEA banquet. I was his date. I spent the evening sitting with Cas Walker, the honored guest speaker, because my date was the president of SNEA and had to be busy the whole evening. A while later, I went out with the SGA president, and he actually stayed in his seat during the meal. I then started dating my husband to be. Anthony and I were both in college. I was in my senior year, and he had just started into college. He was eighteen and I was twenty. He didn't really want to go to college, and I had to work as a student assistant to the Education Department. Anthony would skip class to come by and talk to me. Anthony and I went to church together, and the Lane Theater, and that's about the only places we ever went. He worked part-time at Lawson and Bates Drug Store. When I dated Anthony, we would sit on the porch swing after we got back from the Lane Theater. I had to come straight home after the movie. When 9:30 PM rolled around, even though I was graduating college in May, mom would start flashing the porch light to tell him to leave. Anthony told me he had thought about going over and giving my mom a good night kiss, but he decided not to do that. I'm glad he didn't. Afterward, she would follow me to my room and ask what the movie was about and every detail you could imagine. I was sometimes accused of things that she knew I hadn't done. I was miserable in my own skin. One night, we were planning on going to the Lane Theater, which would finish and get me back home by 9:30 PM. We got to Williamsburg, and something was playing that we didn't want to watch so Anthony came up with the idea to go to Corbin to the Hippodrome Theater. I told him that I would get into trouble as we had no way of letting them know. Cell phones had not yet been invented.

He responded, "Don't worry, I'll go in and explain why we are late." I went along with the plan and worried all through the movie. Keep in mind, Anthony had already asked me to marry him. I just hadn't told them, yet. After the movie, Anthony drove like crazy to get me back home. He went in and explained and neither of my parents said anything. They seemed okay. Anthony left and I headed toward my room. As soon as I started toward my room, mom came behind me. She accused me of things, yelled a bit and I finally just said to her, "Mom, you won't have to worry about that too much longer. As soon as school is out, we are getting married."

She said, "I figured as much. Your dad says I don't have very good control over the girls." I never really understood that remark, but evidently it meant something to them.

I missed my college class the next day. This was the first class I had ever missed in high school or college. I went to college, met Anthony, and we just talked, and I cried. My eyes were swollen shut and I had cried so much. I went home feeling defeated and hopeless. Nothing I could say or do would be right. I just started making plans for the wedding. I knew everything would have to be made by me as I couldn't afford to buy a dress and because I knew they couldn't afford it.

It was early May and I planted flowers for the bouquets, bought fabric to make my dress and veil from money I had earned selling Avon in the evenings, and worked all spring making the dresses, and all that had to be done. My bridesmaid, Sherry Richardson, had her sister make her dress. My younger sister, Diane and Anthony's sister, Cheryl, were the same age; I made their dresses. The only expense that we had besides the fabric was for the cake. We got Mr. Jim Burge, from the Cumberland College cafeteria, to bake our cake. It cost $40. I already had some white shoes. Anthony's uncle George, we called him G.S., served as the best man. My mom's youngest sister, my Aunt Velma sang and her husband, Harry Kegley, played the wedding march and the music for Velma's song. Harry also took the wedding pictures and gave me the negatives. I really felt special to have a family that could do all those things.

I wasn't given any money and we started out with about $200 that we had received for wedding gifts. We had no honeymoon. Our wedding night was spent in Lafollette, Tennessee at Thacker Christmas Inn. Our wedding day was August 3, 1974. Mom griped that week because I wasn't going to be there to help can tomatoes. She complained that I should have at least waited until the canning was done.

Genesis 2:24—*Therefore, shall a man leave his father and his mother, and shall cleave unto his wife: and they shall be one flesh.*

Carolyn West Reaves

Mr. and Mrs. Anthony Reaves

DEATH BY CANCER

In January 1990, the winter had been cold, and my mother had been sick for a while with what she thought was the flu. She had advised us not to come over to visit as she was afraid, we would all end up with the flu. A couple of weeks passed, and she still was sick. When I talked with her on the phone, I urged her to go to the doctor, but she kept telling me she would go when the weather got better. The weeks kept on and she was still sick. During the first week of April, we had a death in the family. My Uncle Tom Taylor had passed away in Fairborn, Ohio and his funeral would be held in Williamsburg. As we gathered at the funeral home that night, I could not believe my mom could look like she did. She looked as if she had been to the Bahamas because her skin had turned completely yellow tan. I urged her to go immediately to the doctor. She assured me that she would go after the funeral was over. A couple of days later she went to the doctor. She probably only went because I kept telling her she needed to go.

My mom was a sixty-year-old woman that never went to the doctor unless she absolutely had to, and she never complained too much about aches or pains. Seeing her in this shape was something I could not have imagined. She usually bounced back quickly when she was sick.

Mom made an appointment with her family doctor, Dr. Scott. After her doctor's visit, I received a call at work informing me that mom was going to the hospital to have emergency gallbladder surgery. I stayed until the school day was over and left as soon as I could to go and be with her. I assumed she would have the surgery and I would see her as she was recovering. The hospital had been performing tests all day instead of doing the emergency surgery. I knew something wasn't right as they still had not taken her back for surgery at the end of the day. They scheduled it for the next morning. When we all arrived at the hospital, she was in surgery, and we had not been told the appointed time had changed. We did not get to see her before her surgery that morning.

A short while later, the surgeon came out and said, "I'm sorry. She had a very large mass on her liver and gallbladder. It was like a brick. It might have been there thirty years or more. She will continue to get weaker and there is nothing we can do for her. We will keep her here for a few days and try to make her comfortable, but she will probably not be going home."

The emotionless report from the doctor still rings in my ears as I think about the state of mind it put each of us in. Everyone started trying to figure out what to do next and lots of tears started falling. We were not prepared to hear news like that, and we immediately started trying to prepare ourselves for going into her room after surgery. She was in recovery and had not been told about this finding. As we each tried to gain composure, it was nearly impossible to find any kind of relief or hope at that moment.

By around 11:00 AM, as we made our way to her room after she was ready to see us, she still was very sleepy and couldn't yet talk with us. She kept watching me as I tried to talk to her. I could tell she knew something was not right as she kept staring at me with her pale blue eyes as if to speak, "Why are you not telling me what I already know?" My sisters, all three of them, took me aside and said: "We think you should be the one to tell her this news." I don't know how they decided it, but they all told me they couldn't do it. I prayed about this and worried that I might say the wrong thing to her.

The next morning my sister, Diane, and I were in my mother's hospital room when Dr. Hamilton came in. He didn't try to sugar-coat the diagnosis. He told her the bad news, but when he told her she didn't cry or do anything like I would have expected. She looked at Dr. Hamilton and said, "I don't think it is my time to die and I am going to fight this thing."

In a few days, she was released to go back home and managed to even attend church two times before she began to get much weaker. My father had always relied so much on her as he worked out in the public and she was a stay-at-home mom. She had been the caregiver for my Grandma West for the last few years of grandma's life. Grandma had passed away in May 1989, just the spring before mom got sick. Mom had no idea she, too, had cancer.

I sat and thought about the final days I had spent with mom at her house and the things she said to me. She said things like, "I want you and Louise to go through that fabric as you two are the only ones that sew." I would talk her out of letting me go through the fabric by saying, "Oh, mom, you will be wanting it back next week." I was trying to make her want to get better, even though we both knew she had only a short time to live. She would see my older sister, Louise, the next day and talk her into sorting the fabric. When I arrived back at mom's house the following day, I had a box of fabric to take home, already picked over by my sister.

Mom didn't like that we had to clean her house, do her laundry, and cook meals for our dad, but she knew it wasn't possible for her to do any of it anymore. After a couple of weeks had passed since she had gotten worse, she would stare for a long time, looking at nothing, and if I said anything to her, she might reply with something like, "There's just so many things to think about." Seeing her in that state was very unusual and it bothered me. I would think about it when I left her house and came home to mine in the evening. Being there every other day, and finally every day for two weeks in the end, was tiring but I felt that I had to be there for her. My husband, Anthony, was working at American Greetings in Corbin, on the night shift. I came home to fix dinner for my girls and would have nobody there to talk to about my day. I was thoroughly depressed about the whole situation, but I never told him that.

Visitors came by mom's house and brought food or cards to make my mom feel better, but she couldn't eat. She did enjoy the cards very much. I would cook plain, bland macaroni for her, and I found some chicken seasoning that I put on it and she liked the taste of it. My mom was a great cook and always made everything without using any recipe. I would think about the many meals she cooked for us every day. When the family came to visit at my mom's, and I was there, I would cook extra so the visiting relatives could eat and share some time with her. We were always taught, for example, to offer a meal to whomever came to visit so the time spent would be more memorable.

As I cleaned her house, I would sometimes find a picture or just something I hadn't seen in a while, and it would take me back to a time in my childhood. I would stop and smile and maybe have a short conversation with her about whatever it was that I had found. Sometimes, even if she had forgotten she had things, and it would take her mind off of her sickness and dread. She would go into detail about the pictures of family or maybe comment about a card she had received from a friend. One day the interim pastor, Benny Bush, came to visit her and they shared a conversation about church and matters that would interest her. I heard mom say to him, "I have not always been the most outspoken Christian in church, but God and I talk a lot here at home." She also stated that her two youngest daughters did not attend church anywhere and she was worried about that.

One day in June 1990, my dad and brothers were working on a house and my dad fell off of the roof and broke his foot. My dad had not been to the doctor in over thirty years for anything. There was no record of tetanus shots or even any penicillin. He suddenly was forced to go to the doctor and be still a few weeks with a cast on his foot. He was much harder to take care of than she was as he wanted to be outside working and the cast forced him to be still and elevate his foot to prevent swelling. Dad had never cooked anything for himself, done laundry, or even washed any dishes that I ever recall. I think the fall was meant for him to stop and take some time to spend with her as this would be her last summer and he hadn't come to terms with that fact. July 4th was soon approaching, and my dad decided he would cook, guided by my mother's direction; he cooked a simple meal of pinto beans and cornbread. My mom couldn't eat it, but he was so proud of his accomplishment and his effort to show my mom that he would be okay when she was no longer there. We all deliberately did not go there that day so they would have the one last holiday together. I still remember the smile he displayed as he told of his meal that turned out "perfect", as he confirmed, as this was his first attempt at cooking. She watched as he talked about the day and how good it had been. It was good to see her smile.

As the end of July came and went, and she steadily began to get weaker, I wondered what I would do if she died while I was alone with her. I could not prepare myself for this one thing as I had never faced anything like this in my life. I was then thirty-seven years old. My husband's grandmother, Maymie, told me her mother died from liver cancer and that it was a horrible death. I didn't want to think about that, but I would think about it every day. I could not imagine how my mother would die and knowing that there was a possibility that her body would force these horrible cancer effects out of her mouth when she died, was too bad to talk about with anyone. I never even told her as I watched her get weaker each day.

School was going to start back the next week, and Louise and I both were teachers. I asked my mom if there was someone in the community, or from the church, that she would want to stay with her during the day while we were at work. She told me not to worry about it. She didn't think she would be here that long and there would be no need.

We were there to visit her on Sunday afternoon, and she tried to speak with my older daughter Clarissa, age 15 at the time. She started a sentence but never finished it. It bothered my daughter very much. She kept wondering what mom was trying to say to her. Clarissa was the oldest grandchild.

I had gone to see mom before I went to work the following Monday, opening professional development day, and when I checked her blood pressure that morning, I could not even get a reading. School was starting that day and I remember wearing a blue dress with a scarf around the neck. My mom commented on how pretty the dress was. Her words were like a whisper because she was so weak.

My sisters were upset with me because I had suggested we take her to the hospital now that she had gotten so much worse. She told us before the disease had spread so rapidly, that she didn't want to go to the hospital to die. I don't think she realized how much pain she would be in before cancer ran its course. By this time, the cancer had really gotten worse, and we were having to take her to Dr. Hamilton every day to have fluid drained from her stomach. The last day I took her, they drained nine liters of fluid from her stomach only to have it back by morning. Her organs were trying to shut down and I knew it was just a matter of time before she would be gone. The last couple of weeks before, she had been so weak and in so much pain at home that I talked with her family doctor about it. He told me she was in the final stages of her cancer. I had to talk with dad alone so that he could face this. He was working near my house, and I drove to the worksite and talked with him.

He looked away with tears in his eyes and said, "I think you're right. We should probably take her to the hospital soon." He didn't take her that day but kept waiting, I think, for some false hope that she would recover.

Mom's uncle, Ed Douglas, in his late 80's, had passed away two days earlier and my brother Roger and I were asked to sing at the funeral. We agreed to do so, and while the funeral was going on, I heard the siren on the ambulance and knew that dad had decided to take her to the hospital. By the time the funeral was over, my mom had already been taken to the hospital in Corbin. I immediately went to the hospital to talk to her. I told her I knew she didn't want to come to the hospital, but I could hardly stand to see her in so much pain. She assured me that it was okay, and the hospital decision was better than staying at home and suffering. She just said in a soft whisper, "this is better." I was so glad she said that to me because as much as I wanted to take her suffering away, I could not, and I felt that having trained medical staff, pain medication, and skilled doctors available, meant everything at that moment in her life. Some of the younger ones didn't understand this and were upset with me because I had talked with dad about this.

August 17th day was sunny and blistering hot. Temperatures were in the high 90's and the humidity were almost unbearable. I looked for a comfortable place in the waiting room to take a quick nap as I didn't want to be too far away in case, I needed to go back to her room. None of us wanted to leave her side. She was taking constant care, and we could come and go as we pleased. Her breathing was labored, and each noise she made as she struggled for breath seemed to be crying out for help.

The death rattle was loud and prominent. I could still hear it inside my head, even when I was away from her. I could not help her, and I felt as though I was letting her down. Just the week before, she very independently made out her bills, arranged phone numbers for family that should be called when she died, and to-do lists for us to take care of. She had asked my sister, Diane, to take dad's suit to the cleaners to have it ready for her funeral. She had always been the organizer and facing death by cancer seemed to just make her want to do more to exercise more independence. I could never have prepared myself to face the storms of life as she did. I would think about that and wonder how hard it must be to lose your desire and ability to do anything else but get ready to die.

As I sat there in the hospital waiting with my brothers and sisters, I was praying for God to go ahead and take her because I could hardly bear to see her in such miserable shape. She was not able to speak or even open her eyes. It was always hard for me to watch anybody in pain, but it was especially hard to see my own mother suffering. My dad was a very strong man that I never saw cry. Just before she passed away, my dad was sitting beside her on her bed in the hospital. He had to make a decision about taking away all the devices that were keeping her alive. I remember seeing the tears start welling up in his eyes and I could see the reflection of her suffering form in his pooling tears. The tears started to fall down his cheeks and he began to sob and asked in a very emotional state, "What should I do?"

I looked at him and said, "It doesn't matter what you decide. It will be the right decision. "

It was at that point I saw my dad start to change. It was as if he had conjured a false hope that he would be taking her home, all fixed up, and back to her usual self. When he had to face the reality of inevitable death, he could not hold back the tears. The man that always was strong in body and spirit now had been forced to make a decision he could barely handle.

I had become so exhausted and could hardly bear to go home and leave her there because the time was so short. I had not talked with anyone about what I feared might happen when she died.

Shortly after 1:00 P.M., I decided to go down to my car and try to get a nap, with the understanding that Anthony would stay in the room with mom, along with my brother Ralph, and my sister-in-law, Juanita. Ralph was the only one of her children remaining in the room at this time. I took Juanita aside before I went downstairs and told her if anything happened, like I had been told might happen, to keep a towel close to mom to cover this up. I knew my mom was such a clean person and would not have wanted to have anyone see her in that state. Juanita assured me she would do this if anything happened. She was the only person I told this to. Juanita has always been as close to me as a sister, sometimes even closer.

Dad went out of the room to go home and rest. My other family members either went home or gathered back in the waiting room and the few people that were in mom's room had only been there alone with her a short while when she died. Juanita was standing by my mom's bedside when it happened, and it happened just as I feared it would. Juanita did as I told her, but it scared her so badly she cried uncontrollably for a long while. We had someone go get dad at his home and bring him back as well as contact other family members that left prior to her death. After the nurses cleaned her up, we were allowed to go in and see her. She looked so peaceful which seemed an impossibility compared to how she looked before as she took her final breaths before she died.

We got the to-do list she had made and called those she wanted to be notified and I went to her house to clean the refrigerator as I knew the food would start coming there from all her friends, family, and neighbors. I felt that I had to take care of things the way she would have done it. Most of the next couple of days was like a blur as we had the visitation on Saturday and the funeral on Sunday. Dad wanted all of us back there on Monday morning to go through her things. I came over and all of my brothers and sisters were there. We had to do this for dad, but it was one of the hardest things I have ever done in my life. Of all the things she organized and listed, what to do with her things and who to give those things to had not been done. Needless to say, it was a very tiring day. We worked until the stars came out that night and decided to come back and finish everything the next day.

People will be so easy to get along with until a death puts everyone in the same room sorting through the things the loved one left behind. I never really had anything in mind that I wanted, but some family members have the reasons all planned out for why he or she should "have it all". I listened and watched as things went here and there. I ended up with a quilt mom had made and hand quilted, but I didn't bring it home. I told my dad I would rather have him use it and I would get it when he died. I left the handmade quilt there with dad. I wish a hundred times over, that I had brought it home then. As things like this often happen, the quilt disappeared. I only found this out after dad passed away, in August 2018.

I had to go back to work at the middle school, where I was an Art teacher, the next day and the grief process had not settled in. I had miserable few months until I decided I had to get a new focus. Everywhere I looked, I was reminded of her, and I missed her. I would look in the mirror while driving and get a glimpse of myself and be reminded of her. I looked a lot like my mom. It was the most depressing days I had ever experienced, up to that portion of my life.

My brothers, sisters, and I did things to stay close and planned for things so we could all enjoy happy times together. We had a cookout at my house on Halloween and we all dressed up in costumes and had a good time. Thanksgiving was the next big holiday and we decided to have something different from the traditional turkey and dressing meal, so we had homemade chili, homemade vegetable soup, and desserts at my house. It was fun but it didn't even seem like we had celebrated the holidays. The winter came and I would think crazy thoughts about snow falling on her grave and I cried a lot when nobody was there. I managed to get through the winter and thought spring would be better after school ended. Spring reminded me of her as she loved the flowers she planted outside. She once had cut a long-stemmed rose from one of our uncle's rose bushes and put it under a canning jar and it grew. It was always so beautiful. There was nothing magical added to it. The winter after mom died, the rose bush died, too. It had been growing there beside my parents' home for more than ten years.

I finally decided that in the summer I would go back to school and change my focus and that is when I began working on my Rank I in School Supervision and Principalship, which were additional endorsements for my career. I was thirty-seven years old at the time. I looked at my mom's age and thought how short the time had been and I tried to think of what my life would be like when I turned 60. Would I be like her, or would I be different? I wanted to make every minute count and count every minute. I still want to put everything I can into each day and not waste a moment of it.

Isaiah 40:31 But they that wait upon the LORD shall renew their strength; they shall mount up with wings as eagles; they shall run, and not be weary; and they shall walk, and not faint.

PAINTING FOR CHURCHES

I recall two different baptistery paintings I completed for churches and several different pictures of churches I have drawn for pastors and others. One baptistery was at Youngs Creek Baptist Church and the other was Goldbug Baptist Church. Both churches are in Whitley County, KY. I worked on them on weekends and each church had their own ideas about how they wanted it to look. The congregation and members seemed to be very proud of the work when it was finished.

I have painted several backdrops for plays, worked on decorations for Vacation Bible School. Those projects take time and effort that most people don't think about. I enjoy doing those kinds of projects, but at a much slower pace than before.

Philippians 3:20–21 — *"For our conversation is in heaven; from whence also we look for the Savior, the Lord Jesus Christ: Who shall change our vile body, that it may be fashioned like unto his glorious body, according to the working whereby he is able even to subdue all things unto himself."*

Goldbug Baptistry

JASON- SUICIDE WAS REAL

I want to include this story because there may be someone that is contemplating ending his or her life and may think that it will only affect them. This chapter may make you think before you commit to suicide. I first met Jason when he was in the seventh grade when I was teaching Art in middle school. Jason was a polite boy, never created any trouble and just smiled as if he was a happy kid. I hadn't seen him in several years when Angelina, my daughter, started dating him and they seemed to go right back to where their friendship left off in high school. Most people tend to only see a few of their former high school friends after high school graduation. Jason had married and divorced. Angelina had done the same. It soon became evident they were going to get married.

Jason had joined the army and Angelina had gone to college off and on and was working full time as a receptionist/secretary for Williamsburg Plastics. She lived less than a mile from her job and Kiersten and Carlee, her daughters, were okay with their mom marrying again.

Their relationship had been rocky at times and Jason was in need of medical assistance due to a back injury he had received when he was serving in the United States Army, stationed in Korea. He had back surgery, but his mental health was suffering. His whole attitude had changed. He felt that he was less than the man he had been before the surgery. He had received counseling and psychiatric treatment via the Veterans Administration, better known as the VA. His moods were not predictable. He sometimes would be upset and leave for weeks at a time. He left before Rafe was born and we were not able to locate him when Angelina went into labor. We finally got word to him through a family member. He arrived at the hospital after Rafe had already made his way into the world. I helped Angelina through her delivery and Anthony talked with Jason as they walked to the car to get her things. He told Jason he had missed the most important day in that baby's life. About a year later, Justice was born. Jason had been gone toward the end of this pregnancy. He would leave and stay at his mom's or other family for a few days but managed to come back home each time. One particular time he went to his family and took the car seats with him, leaving Angelina with no way to transport their small children, which were only two and three at the time. Anthony and I drove to where he was staying and got the car seats and Jason then went back home to Angelina that evening.

I would babysit for them sometimes, but they usually took the small children with them when they went to Lexington for doctor's appointments. They were well-behaved children most of the time.

Trying to get things picked up after Carlee and I had baked a strawberry shortcake and she did homework, I saw the back door open about 8:30PM. It was Jason. Little did I know that less than thirty-six hours later I would be hearing the most horrible words I have ever heard in my life.

I had picked Carlee up from school as Angelina and Jason both had doctor's appointments in Lexington. They had taken the two little ones with them that day and Carlee had been in school.

Anthony and I had both been at work. The evening had been cool, and it felt like it was going to rain.

As Jason walked in, I asked where Angelina and the babies were. He replied, "I left them at the house so she could get them ready for bed." That seemed a bit strange, but I thought maybe they had been hard to handle that day. Lexington is a long trip from Williamsburg with two little ones. Anthony was getting dog food ready and started out the back door. As he started out, Jason followed him, and he looked back and told Carlee to stay inside. I noticed he kept nervously pacing like a cat and I had asked him to have a seat. Each time he refused, stating he needed to get home. Something seemed strange, but I couldn't quite put my finger on it. I speculated in my own mind that they may be arguing, or that the kids were being fussy.

After a while, Carlee got tired of waiting and decided she would put her books in the car. I told her not to bother them as Jason must have been wanting to talk with her papaw. In about twenty minutes Anthony came back in and he was alone. I asked where Jason and Carlee were, and he told me they had left. Curious about Jason's following him outside, I asked what the conversation was about that took so long.

Anthony replied, "He just wanted to say he was sorry for all he had ever put us through; that we were good people and didn't deserve what we were dealing with." I paused and wondered why he would say those things. There has been no exchange of unkind words recently. In the short few minutes, he was inside, he had told me that he was planning on working on those old cars parked near their place and getting them running. He talked of plans like he was enthusiastic about getting them going again.

I arrived at work on Thursday about 9:00 AM and I knew I had class at 9:25 AM. On the way to work I thought about all the things I would get done that day and then my cell phone rang as soon as I parked my car. It was Angelina. She was at work in the Corbin area and said she was having trouble with Jason that morning. As she kept talking, I asked the usual questions, "Is everything okay?" "What can we do?" and then I told her I had class in a few minutes and students were waiting on me and I had another class following that one. I told her I would get back with her at lunch. It is hard to wear the Mom hat and the Instructor hat at the same time.

I got busy at work and didn't call her at lunch, but Anthony talked with her, and Jason was having a bad day. He was using bad language and was arguing with Carlee, Angelina's then 10-year-old, from a previous relationship. Carlee was told to clean her room. She had taken the broom into her bedroom. Jason wanted it and she told him she would give it to him when she got finished. He didn't like her attitude, didn't like anything at all about his day, and didn't think he should take orders from a 10-year-old. Needless to say, he was not going to take it today and he thought everyone was against him.

Anthony spoke with Angelina on his way home and the heated attitude was getting worse. I had gone to Faber Baptist Church at 7:00 PM to practice singing as we were scheduled to sing in Pineville on Sunday. We had just set up our equipment, practiced one song, and I saw the church door swing open.

It was Kiersten, Angelina's eldest child, and she was crying uncontrollably. I hugged her and asked what was wrong. My heart was racing and trying to imagine all kinds of things that might have happened, but not this. She was sobbing so hard she could not talk. I finally heard, "Jason......killed......himself!"

I went numb and at first, I thought I had misunderstood. She offered to take me in her car, but I had my car at the church, so she rode with me. My brother Roger and friends Darryl and Jim told me to go on and they would put the equipment away and lock it up. I had been to the heart doctor the week before and was wearing a heart monitor. I am sure the heart monitor was not reading accurately. The rain was pouring down, and it was as if the skies were crying with us.

Anthony and I had to go to Jason's parents' house and tell them the bad news. Jason's parents lived on a farm, situated way out in the country; with the darkness and the rain, we had to stop and ask directions. When we arrived, I stayed in the truck. I watched as the rain kept splattering all over the windshield and saw Jason's dad come to the door. He just dropped his head and kept listening as Anthony told him what happened. I could only just imagine how hard it was going to be for him to tell Jason's mother, who had already gone to bed at that time. Anthony came back to the car, and we talked about all kinds of things going back to our house. When we got home, there were preachers, church members, and family all over the place at my house. I just sat on the porch and tried to stay as calm as I could. Some came out and talked with us, but I can't even remember any of the conversation. The kids were aware that something was not right, but they didn't know what was wrong. I remember one thing that Rafe, age 3 at the time, said about a week after this tragedy. He asked, "Would there be screaming in heaven"?

1 John 1:9—*If we confess our sins, he is faithful and just to forgive us [our] sins, and to cleanse us from all unrighteousness.*

Jason Lester

DAD'S CONVERSATION ABOUT BLACK STAR

After dad was diagnosed with Alzheimer's Disease, he would often talk about the days he worked in the Black Star Coal Mines in Alva, Kentucky. This was in Harlan County. He started working there when he was about seventeen. He told of the first day at work he was handed a shovel and pick and had to dig the coal out of that mountain and how they started out with very little. Their neighbors were like family. They had no car, and my dad didn't even know how to drive. He and mom would ride the bus to Williamsburg and beyond, to visit family, or they would get a ride from "the Suttons" who also lived close by. He fondly recalled his acquaintances there and told how he got the job. Uncle Harold West, his brother, already was working there and he helped get dad a job. He, Uncle Harold, and a cousin Elvis Cornelius lived in a boarding house together. Dad worked there from 1948 until 1956.

<u>Jeremiah 6:16</u> — *Thus, saith the Lord, Stand ye in the ways, and see, and ask for the old paths, where is the good way, and walk therein, and ye shall find rest for your souls.*

Black Star Coal Corporation

A CALL TO SERVE

Have you ever wondered what it is like to know that God has appointed you to do a work, but you do not feel ready to answer the call? We sometimes think we are not worthy of God's love, and we listen to the wrong voices and find ourselves in a miserable state. Anthony, my husband, had not really been saved when he, as a child, went forward at the altar call and followed in baptism. He has stated in his testimony that he only went forward at church to make his parents and grandparents proud of him. He lived a double life, so-to-speak, in front of his family, the people he worked with, and even in front of me, his wife. He had never told me about this; I just assumed he was already saved. We attended a revival service at Wofford Baptist Church, in April.

1982, at the invitation of Anthony's Aunt Estele Kinder, and a neighbor, Mike Frazier. Mike was completing student-teaching at the middle school where I taught. Mike had met with me a couple of times during Spring Break to practice singing so that I could do my first solo in church. I had never sung a solo before, but I had played the piano for a youth group at our former church, Jellico Creek Baptist Church, where Anthony and I were married and where I had been a member since I was 12 years old.

The revival was underway and there were many people there that I had never met, but there were enough there that I knew made me less nervous. The visiting evangelist preached after the special singing and Rev. Bart Powers, the pastor, welcomed everyone. After the visiting evangelist brought a message, the altar call went out and nobody went to the altar. Rev. Powers said he felt that someone still was trying to bargain with the Lord and asked for another song. At that point, Anthony went to the altar. I was not sure what was going on because I thought Anthony was a Christian. I had no reason to think otherwise. Anthony never participated in drinking or any other thing that we associate with people who are not Christians. I joined him in prayer and asked that the Lord help Anthony with whatever it was that was disturbing him. When the prayer was finished, Anthony announced to the congregation that he had just gotten saved. The revival then started showing on the faces of many of those that were there. One man said the service was the best he had ever attended. I moved my membership there to support Anthony and our family. I saw a change in Anthony's whole demeanor immediately and I knew it was God.

After the week of revival, Vernon Reynolds approached me and asked if I would like to have him play the guitar for me the next time I decided to sing. I told him that we could try it. I then told him about my brother, Roger West, and his guitar playing abilities. We agreed to pray about it, and I talked with Roger and asked if he would be interested in trying this. We met and really were blessed to have Vernon Reynolds as a part of our little group. We sang there quite a bit, even though Roger was not a member there. Our eldest daughter, Clarissa, was saved at home and was later baptized at this church.

We later started going to Mountain Ash Baptist Church, at the request of one of my students. We enjoyed the services, and it allowed us to meet more Christians and fellowship with them. As time went on, Angelina, our younger daughter, was saved and got baptized in this church. We stayed there for a few years. My brother, Roger, and I recorded a video and cassette tape there. The video was played on the local television broadcast from the church several times that year and the church sold many cassette tapes. After mom passed away, we started going to church at Goldbug Baptist as it was closer and my brother, Roger, was attending this church. Anthony knew when we were at Mountain Ash that he had been called to preach, but he only told me. He told me not to discuss this with anyone, not even his mother. I kept quiet. I could not understand it, but I didn't question his decision.

At the end of the school year, 1991, I decided to go back to school to change my focus and to help further my career. After losing a mom, I needed something else to keep me going and to fight the depression I was suffering after losing her. I finished my administration schooling, passed the necessary tests, and started looking for a new job as principal or assistant principal. I interviewed in my home district, as well as several other neighboring districts when a job opening came about. Each time, I would find that I was a formality, only satisfying the need to have a few candidates go through the motions, to be told that someone else got the job. People would anonymously call and tell me not to go to the interview as "so and so" already has been told they will get the job. As I ignored the messages and interviewed, the decisions made were exactly as the unidentified caller had predicted. I finally decided that this was enough and went outside of the local area and started applying in other places. I applied for a job in Hazard, KY. It was a job for assistant principal of Roy G. Eversole Intermediate and Middle School. Five candidates applied and I got hired for the job. I began there in September 1994. I worked so hard trying to please everyone. I had to begin work as soon as I could be released from my contract in Whitley County. I had to rent an apartment in Hazard, and stay through the week, then go home on the weekend. Fortunately for me, one of the teachers at the school, Alexis Cornett, had an apartment that was less than a mile from the school and it was furnished. I paid $300 per month, and she included all utilities.

Three weeks after I had been there, Louise, my older sister, called and told me that she was very sick and described pain such as that of gallstones. I had already dealt with gallstones and urged her to go to the doctor immediately as our mother had died from complications from gallbladder and liver cancer just four years previously.

She told me she would make an appointment and get it checked out. She made the appointment and on the day of the surgery, I couldn't be there as I had just started this new job. She assured me she would be okay and that they would call me when the surgery was over. I waited for the call, and I didn't receive one. By the end of the day, I was getting worried. As I walked up the hallway of the school, about 3:00 PM that afternoon, some students were waiting to be picked up. I saw my husband walking in the front door of the school. He had been at work in Corbin at American Greetings and my family called him and asked if he would go tell me what was happening. This drive was about an hour and a half from Corbin.

When I saw Anthony, I knew something terrible was wrong. He informed me that Louise's liver was completely covered with cancer and that she only had a short time to live. What could I do at that moment but cry out to God to help me again? I made the drive home that evening to see her. She had been on a medical leave the previous school year due to having breast cancer. Her level of depression was rock bottom. I wanted to help her, but how could I do anything for her.

I said to her, "If I had known you were this sick, I would not have taken this new job."

Her reply to me was, "No, you did the right thing. You are going to need this job to take your mind off of your troubles." I had never lost a sister before and I didn't know what to do as I had no idea what would happen to her children or her husband. Her husband had known her since grade school.

I had election day off the first Tuesday in November. Before I came home, I called her and then went home to Williamsburg. After I arrived, I contacted her to make a meal for her. She told me she thought she could eat some roast, potatoes, green beans, and peach pie. I made the chosen meal and took it to her home. Her daughter, Amie, then a sophomore in high school, and Tommy, a seventh grader and H.C., her husband, were the only people at the table. Everyone was quiet except for their forks occasionally touching the plate to take a mouthful of food. She got up from the table, without eating, and said to us that the noise was too much for her. She went and got back into bed. I felt really bad for her children because I knew they were going to feel what I had felt when I lost my mother, except they would feel it at a much younger age.

She passed away on November 15, 1994, and her birthday would be on November 29. She would have been 43 on her birthday. The school year dragged on, but she was later awarded an honor posthumously. I went with her children and husband to accept it in her honor. The award was presented at Campbellsville College, and it was "Teacher of the Year". I remember how proud those kids were of their mom and how sad it was that the award came after she had passed away. The tears were flowing because they were so proud of their mom, and they had to accept this in her absence.

Anthony had grown up in church all his life. Two generations of grandfathers and his father were all Baptist preachers, and Anthony felt like he would drop the tradition and just be a Sunday

School teacher, of the middle-school-aged boys, probably. In his heart, he knew that this was not what God wanted and he tried to run from the calling as he had seen some of the things his father had dealt with in the past. Satan tried to convince him this would be okay. We were attending Goldbug Baptist Church and the pastor had recently resigned. Anthony was serving on the pulpit committee. The pulpit committee was responsible for making sure there would be a visiting preacher for the services on Sunday. On one Sunday, at Goldbug Baptist Church, the pulpit committee had made a mistake and there was no preacher there to bring a sermon. The ladies' Sunday School class met in the back in the fellowship hall and the men's class met in the front part of the church. After Sunday School, I sat down in the general area where we usually sat and waited for Anthony to come over and join me. Our little granddaughter, Kiersten, then three, was there sitting beside me. When he came over, he was acting nervous, scrambling through his bible, and proceeded to tell me that he would be bringing his first message that morning. I didn't question it as I knew what his secret had been for quite some time. I told Kiersten, "You will need to be very quiet; papaw is going to be the preacher."

Her mom, Angelina, came out of her Sunday School class and joined us. Kiersten said, "Mommy, papaw is going to be the creature today!" Of course, we all laughed about that later. Anthony had to come clean with the congregation about his calling and proceeded to preach his first sermon without any pre-planned sermon notes. That afternoon, Anthony read his bible and I kept to myself as he prepared for the evening sermon. That evening, his dad and mom came to hear him preach. Goldbug eventually got a pastor and Anthony was ordained to preach. His first church to pastor was Patterson Creek Baptist church. I continued to work in Hazard, trying to get closer home. I had been promoted to Supervisor of Schools and continued until I had five years of time completed there. Two weeks after

Anthony had preached, I got a job offer closer home at McCreary County Preschool. I left my job as Supervisor of Schools in Hazard City Schools and took a huge pay cut to come home to be supportive of Anthony's surrender to the call to preach. I stayed in McCreary County Schools for five years. I served as the preschool principal and District Supervisor. After medical leave the last year, I retired in 2004.

A year after retirement from the public-school system, I applied to work at the University of the Cumberlands. This is where I earned my undergraduate degree. I was hired to work as a secretary, minimum wage, for the Academic Resource Center. This is the resource on campus referred to as the ARC. Peer tutoring takes place and students can have a place to study.

The following year Dr. Larry Cockrum, now the President of the University of the Cumberlands, spoke to me to see if I would be interested in becoming the Director of the program. I accepted the offer to continue in my calling, that of serving others. I also started teaching Art Appreciation and Study Skills. I was hired in September 2006 and every day is different, but I still enjoyed working in this environment. I tried to begin each of my classes with prayer and have prayed many times with college students when they have come to me in need of prayer. They have also comforted me with prayer when I needed it.

His calling to my life has taken me much farther than I thought I would go when I graduated and got married in 1974. He has continually blessed and provided for my needs every day. I could not be here writing this if God was not directing my path.

I have tried to be a supportive wife, singing in church, playing the piano for the congregation, singing in surrounding area churches in a group called, "The Trinity Trio", and being the leader of the Women on Mission group at churches we have been members of.

Being in the back behind everyone else is a hard place to be. Anthony knows I always stand behind him in his work for the Lord and he does for me. We make a good team. There is just something about being married and seeing each other every day that lets me know when things are bothering him, even when he doesn't tell me. I can see it in his facial expressions and how he walks. When he is troubled, it shows in his eyes. The call to serve does not just refer to church work. It should be part of our everyday life. When a family is sick, it should be our duty to help with that. Recently, my dad, Allen West, became unable to be left alone due to complications from Alzheimer's Disease. Each of his children agreed to help with his needs. We all understood that his disease was progressing quickly and each of us helped with different needs. He eventually became combative and wanted to try and leave several times during the night.

We searched for a place that offered skilled care, 24 hours each day and found that at Laurel Heights, in London, KY. It was not a pleasant task, but we felt that it was the best thing we could do for him because he was not able to sleep well at home and was not eating very much. When he didn't understand why he had to take a shower, or why he had to have people there taking care of him, he would become aggressive. He oftentimes was confused about who we were and had forgotten that his brothers and a sister, as well as his eldest daughter, were no longer living. The care he received there was excellent. He often commented about how good the food was. I was able to go see his needs every day. I went to visit him every day, except two. Those were Saturdays.

He was never even aware he was in a nursing facility. He thought he was in the hospital.

His last words to me before he died on Friday evening. He said, "I'm going home in the morning." I believe he did go home to be with my mom, his parents, and two children in heaven. His stay was 12 days and even though some members of the family condemned me and two of my brothers to the lake on fire for helping to get him into this facility without telling them, they are wrong. Full cooperation was not being given and trail cameras installed in the garage and in the house without the permission of dad, or my bother that had the power of attorney for dad, led to a breakdown of communication and trust among all the family members. I have no regrets about finding great care for him. I grieve for him, too, but I can sleep at night knowing he is no longer suffering.

<u>Matthew 12:18</u> — *"Behold, my servant whom I have chosen; my beloved in whom my soul is well-pleased; I will put my spirit upon him, and he shall proclaim justice to the gentiles."*

Patterson Creek Baptist Church.

SPECIAL PEOPLE WE HAVE MET AT CHURCHES

I could never have made it in this life without family and friends. I especially will fondly remember people from the various churches I have been associated with. Anthony and I were married at the Jellico Creek Baptist Church in 1974 and fondly recall many people from there that have gone on to heaven. I remember there were many such as Fred and Opal Shelley, Rev., and Mrs. Charlie Taylor, many of the Meadors, Marion and Nannie Wilson, Bill and Shirley Lester, Sol and Minnie Cox, Edith, and Frank Swain, and so many more.

From Wofford Baptist Church, I remember Donald Jones leading the singing, JoAnn Siler, and her mother Gladys Tolliver, Aunt Estele Kinder, the Fraziers', Rev. Bart Powers, and his brother T. J. Powers, and many more.

From Mtn. Ash Baptist Church, I remember Darlene and Billy Carpenter and their family, Robert, and Pam Coker, Verendra Sharp, Truman Lawson, Jan, and Ted Surber and lots of young people that were students of mine in middle school.

We later joined Goldbug Baptist Church, and I remember Willard Foley leading the singing, his wife Louise writing and singing songs, standing beside Coy Bledsoe's wife, in the choir, along with the Shelleys, Wayne and Jean Prewitt, and the Logans, Brian and Janet.

After Anthony announced his call to preach, we were led to Patterson Creek Baptist Church where I met Lavonne Reynolds, Junie McKiddy, George and Eleanor Monhollen, Dot and Billie

Baker, Thelma McWilliams, Jarvis and Noba Smith, Mary Cureton, Jessie Smith, Joann Young, Billy Rickett, Judy Lawson, and Harold Rickett, just to name a few. We served there for 10 years.

We then were led to Faber Missionary Baptist Church. We served there for a little over 13 years. We met many devoted Christians there. My husband always tried to schedule activities that appealed to all the different ages.

Some of the best services I have attended have been those that consisted of people audibly giving their testimonies. Some of the testimonies have touched my heart strings and often come to mind when I am feeling down. The service is usually informal and very welcoming. Singing in churches with The Trinity Trio gave me a purpose and allowed me to hear others sing and testify. Witnessing souls come to the Lord during a service is especially heartwarming.

John 15:13— *Greater love hath no man than this, that a man lay down his life for his friends.*

Faber Baptist Church

DINNER WITH A STRANGER

Visiting my dad used to be just a time I took for granted. When our girls were younger, and mom was still alive, we sometimes would let them spend the night at their grandparents' house. They sometimes remember little games my mom would play with them, but they never really ever mentioned dad doing anything special with them. That was basically how I remembered my life growing up. I remember everyone always being quiet at the dinner table except mom and dad. If we looked at each other and started to laugh, we were told to leave the table.

Mom had cancer and passed away in August 1990. Dad had to learn to do things for himself and he never really depended upon any of his kids to do anything for him, until recently. When mom passed away, he was still working out in the public with my brothers and after a short while after her death, he started dating. He never married again and that is a blessing, in more ways than one. We didn't visit dad much because his lady friend and her brother were usually there, or he had gone to her house.

About four years ago, dad was diagnosed with Alzheimer's disease and required many new demands in order for him to stay in his own home without going to the nursing home. My five living brothers, sisters and I have each taken turns, on a schedule, taking meals for his supper and spending the night at his home. He didn't eat very much, except for dessert. He did love sweets. We have all tried to cook things that are healthy, but he was quick to let me know he liked "Arsh" fried potatoes better than anything. Arsh is how the southern people refer to Irish, white, Kennebec potatoes. I know what he means, but others may not. At the dinner table, the conversation was basically the same every day. He couldn't remember where I worked most of the time. He thought I still worked in the public schools, in McCreary County. I hadn't worked in McCreary County since 2004 and I have worked at University of the Cumberlands since 2006. He told me about his first job, living in the boarding house, and how hard the labor was back then. He said he really liked working there. They didn't have telephones, and if one of the neighbors needed something, they would throw a rock and hit the side of the house and alert my mom and dad for a cup of sugar or something.

He has told me of his remedy for some pesky neighbor kids riding on the fence and trying to break the boards. He asked them to get off of the fence. They did something I would never have done. They ignored his request. He took a large bucket of water and threw it on them. They left mad and yelled, "I will tell my dad on you!"

Dad's reply was, "Go get him; I don't care." He reinforced the fact that he dealt with the matter. He never said anything about what mom did during their time there. I wonder how she managed to be far away from her mother and family, in McCreary County, especially after she was pregnant with her first child. I sometimes think about something mom said about his attitude when they first married. For unknown reasons to me, he made her burn her old high school books, and pictures of her friends. She didn't explain why he did this, but she almost always did what he told her. Knowing about this explains a lot to me about why she seemed so frustrated at times.

I want to back up in my story and tell you about him before Alzheimer's became so confining. He used to like to go listen to Roger and me sing if the churches were close by. He could still drive and wasn't depending on anybody to get him to the church.

He knew his way around and would be there on time for everything. One Saturday night, about four years ago, I had just fallen asleep, and I heard the telephone ring. I got up and answered the phone. It was Juanita asking us to come and help search for dad. He had been to see his "girlfriend" and left around 10:00 PM. It was now close to 1:00AM and he had not gotten home. We went in different directions looking for him. The rain was pouring down and with every drop that fell, our thoughts of finding him dead or never finding him at all were beginning to take over. As the night hours creeped into morning, around 2:00AM the Williamsburg City Police Dispatch received a call that he had been located in Knoxville, Tennessee. He had gotten on the interstate by mistake as it was pouring the rain and possibly, he just followed the taillights of the car in front of him. He knew where he was and knew he needed to head back north but didn't know how to get back on I-75 North to go home. The officer that stopped to assist him on the side of the road, thought he was probably an old man out drinking. When he looked at his license and realized he was an 83-year-old man, he would not let him drive back home. He was sober and had never drank in his life, I know of. My brothers Roger and Ralph went to Knoxville to get him and found him happily chatting with the officers in the police station, eating cookies, and drinking coffee. After the long ride home, my brothers ended up staying up with him until 6:00 AM trying to make sure he was okay and that he would not be driving after dark.

Dad usually sat on the front porch with mom in the evening after supper when we were growing up. There was an old porch swing that was the special sitting place for mom and dad. The television only had one channel as we never had cable when I grew up. We never ate out in a restaurant. Dad would sometimes take us for a ride to Williamsburg and he would let mom go in and get a bucket of

Kentucky Fried Chicken on a Sunday afternoon. I don't remember ever eating out any other times. We would sometimes visit with our grandparents on Sunday afternoon. Visits to our grandparents on the West side of the family usually ended up in conversation of work that we would be helping them with. We helped with gardening, stripping tobacco, commercial chicken houses, breaking up green beans, staying with the grandparents as they started aging, and helping gather apples. Grandma usually had some clothes hanging on the clothesline that needed folding and we helped with that, too.

I remember when I was a child how dad's temper would rage at times, but he usually only stayed mad for a short time. When I was about 14, in the late part of Fall, I noticed the way mom and dad were not speaking to each other at the table. It seemed that every click of a fork on a plate sounded like an echo in the kitchen. This went on for nearly three weeks. Short answers and daily routine of packing lunches by mom followed by him going on to work and the kitchen dishes left ready to be washed. I remember asking mom why he was so upset. Her answer startled me as I hadn't thought about this being an issue to make a parent upset. She told me she thought she might be pregnant. At that time, I didn't understand too much about how that could have happened, but I was pretty sure it took both of them to be there. After about nine months, July 30, to be exact, our youngest sister was born. Pam was spoiled by all of those in the family. Louise was then 16; I was 14; All of the others were as stair steps down to Diane, the youngest which had just turned 6 when Pam was born.

Conflict resolution usually consisted of mom and dad arguing behind closed doors, with dad being the only raised voice heard. We were told to stay in another room or go outside. I never questioned dad about anything, but I always did ask mom when things were not going right. Dad never wanted us to have anything we didn't earn. I recall one Easter weekend when I was young; we made a trip to McCreary County to visit my Grandparents. My Uncle Orville Perkins and some others were there for the weekend. Plastic Easter eggs were just coming out and that is the first time I ever remember seeing those. Orville and Gloria never had any children of their own and they sometimes would bring gifts, such as puzzles, for us to enjoy. This Easter was special because they had placed some change in the plastic eggs and had hidden them in Grandpa's field. Upon hearing about the plastic eggs, we ran to find the hidden treasures. As we picked each one up and rattled it to listen to the loose change inside, we would get excited. When we finished the egg hunt, dad made us give the change back to our uncle. We did what we were told but we were embarrassed to do so. The drive back home was quiet. We didn't dare ask why for fear of hearing him get upset.

He would have a certain look on his face, and you would know that he was angry.

I don't ever recall dad getting too involved with us as kids. We had chores to do and helped with whatever task was at hand. Mom always cooked a big breakfast of bacon, eggs, gravy, and biscuits.

While Louise helped mom make breakfast, I made the beds and set the table. My brothers helped feed our cattle and pigs. We got ready for school, with only one bathroom, and rode the school bus to the elementary school. Everything at school was pretty much routine. We didn't have enough students to have a basketball team, football team or cheerleaders. We didn't have a gym. On rainy days or cold days, we stayed inside and did artwork or read books. Sometimes a checkerboard would be brought out and games would go on with the winner playing the next person in line to compete. We had spelling tests on Friday and every morning started with songs from the students. Students could sing while the teacher got the lessons ready to present. Three grades were all together in the same room for 6th-8th grades. We were all like family. In the Spring, we would bring jump ropes, basketballs, softballs, and bats to play with at school. I remember mom taking our old bobby socks and unraveling them and forming a ball for us to use. Someone had knocked the softball we had been using into high weeds and we were not able to get to it. Sometimes, someone would bring horseshoes and we would have competitions with those. There were no overweight students that I recall. Chubby maybe, but not overweight. We didn't have a lunchroom, and everyone brought their lunch. We would sometimes trade food with friends and just have fun.

As dad's Alzheimer's disease got worse, we had to make some tough decisions. We watched as his demeanor changed and he began to sleep more during the day. Most of the time he was cooperative, at first. As time went on, he would get up in the night and get fully dressed and head toward the back door, several times during the night. We had installed alarms, but he couldn't remember that. Sometimes he would get there before we could keep him from setting off the alarm but many times he would get up, turn the alarm off, and go back to bed only to repeat this scenario at least three more times during the early hours of the morning. He would say, "Boy, that thing is loud!" and we would agree with him.

He usually did what we asked him to if we said, "Dr. Williams wants you to do this or that." He liked Dr. David Williams, his physician in Williamsburg, and laughed and told us over and over how he had a doctor's appointment with Dr. Williams and when the doctor was examining him, he told the doctor, "Don't be examining and looking for too much—I'm not getting ready to join the army, now." Dad was 87 at the time and thought that was one of the funniest things he had ever said.

He couldn't remember things like where I work, anyone's birthday except his own, that my eldest sister passed away in 1994, and that some of his own brothers and sisters are no longer living, or that they don't own the homes they once had near him. He recently saw people getting Christmas decorations out of the garage at the home his sister, Eula, once owned. He walked up to the house and told the people to get out of there. He informed them he had been watching them and had seen them in that garage. He thought his sister still lived there and those were her things. Actually, she passed away almost two years before that. The neighbors told him they had bought the house. He then turned and told them he would go back home. He just walked back and didn't bother them further.

As things started to get really confusing for him, Ralph and Roger went to see dad and discussed how it would be better for Roger to have the checkbook so he could take care of immediate bills instead of all of his transactions being done with cash. It was okay for dad to have some cash in his wallet, but he couldn't remember what he was doing with his money or how much of it he was spending. Dad understood and willingly gave the checkbook to Roger. Later that evening, he called Ralph just a short time after supper, and told him to bring the checkbook back. Ralph explained that he didn't have it. He and Roger went to see dad again that evening and dad never even mentioned it. The brothers went back home with the checkbook.

The very next day, he called and wanted the checkbook back again. This time, they took it to him and then Ralph made a visit to his "girlfriend" and after some exchange of accusations and harsh words, Ralph went home. Money was going out of dad's checking account every month, but nothing could show where it was being spent. It was impossible for dad to tell anyone why $400 or $500 was being written in the form of a check made out to 'cash' and nothing showing for what was being bought.

After a few months of this, we had another meeting. This was at Ralph's as he was at home after his accident, and everyone could meet there. We were given our schedule and prompted to start this immediately.

We each were given bed linens and a blanket to put on the bed we would be sleeping in while we stayed at dad's. We changed the bed when we got up and left the mattress ready for the next one to spend the night. Kayla, Pam's daughter, spent the day with him and was paid $100.00 per day, Monday through Friday, from 7:00AM to 5:30PM. If she had to have a day off, she usually arranged for Jerry to spend time there while she was away. We had a schedule for every day of the week, and we tried to keep everything running as smoothly as possible. Ralph was supposed to be contacted if there was a change in the schedule for whatever reason. Sometimes they just made other arrangements but didn't tell Ralph.

Before we started this new schedule idea, dad was staying alone at night, but he was staying up until about 11:00 PM because he had night visitors, which caused him to sleep all day. Dr. Williams told him he needed to get into bed earlier, so he got in bed most nights from about 8:00 to 9:00 PM. Sometimes he slept until 11:00 PM and tried to get up, get dressed and thought he had slept all night. Most nights he went to bed and might get up a few times during the night and then he would get up to stay around 5:00 AM. On Saturday night, he usually stayed up later, because he had night visitors until late. His mood was sometimes not too good on Sunday, especially in the evening.

We no longer have family gatherings at dad's. We quit having them about four years ago as things were not the same. There were no reasons to celebrate with family as it was said that dad did not want to do it anymore. Well, most of us didn't know when dad was celebrating. He had a tree and he later talked about opening gifts with Phyllis and her brother Joe. He never would open the gifts we gave him in front of us and never knew who gave him the gifts.

The day after Christmas 2017, before we started the schedule of spending the night there, he got up around 5:00 in the morning, managed to go outside, without a coat. It was really cold and a neighbor driving to an early shift of work saw dad just wandering around across the road. He didn't have any shoes or socks on, and his coat was missing. He was also dripping wet because he had fallen into the stream of water by stumbling into it because he was disoriented. That neighbor managed to get my dad to my cousin, Darrel West, that just lives about a half a mile from my dad's place. An emergency call was made, and an ambulance was called for. He was given some dry clothes to wear and was covered with quilts. This was what let us know dad had reached another stage in his illness. He ended up in the hospital with a diagnosis of Septic Shock. His fever was high, he had infection and had to have antibiotics administered through an IV. He was within minutes of death at that point.

He stayed in the hospital for about a week. We started the mandatory schedule as soon as we brought him home. Our whole lives changed. We had to put alarms on the doors so he wouldn't try to leave during the night. We each had to jump out of bed to keep him from going out the door at night, usually between 2:00 to 5:00 AM.

After he had been home only a few days, he ended up with a really bad case of the flu. I took him to Dr. Williams, and they did a "swab" test of his nose and throat. Both tests came back negative, even though he was running a fever. They thought he probably had a urinary tract infection. They also wanted to rule out pneumonia, so they asked me to take him to Corbin to the diagnostic center. They did a chest x-ray, and we took him back home. He kept thinking he was going to have to throw up. He managed to not do that. That was on Friday. That night Anthony and I had to stay with him. He got up during the night, fell out of the bed twice, urinated on the floor, then on Anthony and didn't want to get up out of the floor. By morning, after taking Tylenol, his fever was still around 102.6. I told all those at dad's by then, "We have to take him to the emergency room. He has to have something wrong with him. We can't get his fever to go down."

Anthony and my brother Jerry helped him get into the shower, then we took him to the emergency room at Baptist Hospital in Corbin. We arrived there a little before 11:00 AM. They did some tests and at about 2:00 PM, they came in and confirmed he had the flu. Dad got admitted to the hospital. Roger had already been sick with it and could not be there to admit him. Roger had the power of attorney, so he came over to the hospital, wearing a hospital mask, signed the necessary papers and he got dad admitted. Dad was so "giving" that day. He ended up giving Anthony, Diane, Jerry, and me the flu. I was so glad he was in the hospital getting some attention there. We could not go to work, so it gave us a few days to get over it. I was still on our scheduled holiday break, and this was the last week of it, another blessing from God.

His dog, Andy, was sick and seemed to be getting worse. We would have to hear it gag during our meals, during the night as the dog was allowed to sleep in the back of the kitchen, near the guest bedroom. Needless to say, we could not sleep. After several weeks of hearing the groans, and gagging of the dog, Anthony and I had a conversation with dad about the dog being sick. He agreed for us to take the dog to the local veterinarian, Dr. Culver. He ran tests on the dog, gave him a shot of penicillin, steroids, and other medications to see if he would get better. The dog had heart worms and being around 14 years old was not going to insure full recovery. His medication was given religiously for eight days. He had gotten worse, so Anthony and I took Andy back to the same clinic two weeks later. Before I went, I talked with dad and told him that the dog may not be well enough to come back home. He agreed to have the dog 'put down' if that was the case. I dreaded it but I was pretty sure this would be the case. I had also asked dad if he wanted to bring the dog back home to bury it or leave it with the doctor. He told me to leave it there.

As each week passed, he seemed to change more in his demeanor. He could not understand why, in his words, "Everyone is moving in and trying to tell me what to do." He would not flush the commode and didn't want others to because he thought it was wasting water, even though his water was well water and there was never a bill for that. He didn't want my brother, an accountant, to pay to have a line devoted to the internet installed, which would allow Roger to work on taxes on nights/days he is staying with dad. He wanted to know "Why we were all coming there because he didn't need anybody there". He used some harsh language, cursed, and shook his fist in my brother's face and told us to leave. Roger had no choice but to stay with him that night. After all, he was scheduled to be there for dad. After things settled back down, I went home after trying to reason with him unsuccessfully. This was the second time he had been violent toward Roger, and eventually toward me. Each time was after he had visitors on Saturday night until way past his usual bedtime. This routine was unnecessary and was of no benefit to him.

A phone call was made to Dr. Williams and new medication changes were made the very next day. I picked up his prescription and we gave him the new medication in the evening after his meal. I did not feel like fixing my hair that day and I pulled it up, secured it with a clip in the back. While having dinner he looked over and asked me something that I would never have believed. He said, "Did you get a perm?"

I answered him, "No, but I need one, and have an appointment for that in the morning". What was unusual about that is that he has never in my life said anything about my hair before. I couldn't laugh about it then, but I thought about it later and laughed out loud just thinking about it. I really think he thought I was somebody else.

I know he got very hateful toward the others, but some never share it with me, so I do not include that in this chapter. Some stones are better left unturned.

We were writing down, on a check off sheet, when his medications and meals were given and which family member was there to complete the task, but some of them would never communicate for whatever reason. It was the same when all family members, after meeting together three times, were asked to sign a promissory note listing how much money they owed dad for land or monetary assistance he had given in the past. A promissory letter was addressed to each of my brothers and sisters asking for this matter to be taken care of. Dad can't remember anything about it and the ones that owe him money are the ones that have not filled the paper out and signed it.

Dad tried to stay awake until about 8:30 PM on the night when I was there. The reason is that he has stayed up really late the night before because his "lady friend" and her brother come over on nights when Roger or I are not scheduled to be there. I have never said anything to her about her stay, but I did tell dad in front of her that his doctor said he needed more rest. It was not a lie, and I was trying to be kind. She heard it and ignored it. She usually left around 11:00 PM and then he wanted to sleep off and on all day. As a result, as soon as supper was over, he started wanting to go to bed and wants us to go to bed, too.

Later, he was sitting there in the kitchen, and I found something on the television I was interested in, and he looked over at 8:15 PM and said, "Go ahead and turn the TV off. I'm not watching it. We all can just go to bed." It reminded me of when I was in college. I went to school all year long. When school was over in the spring, reruns were on which meant I got to watch a show for the first time. Dad and mom would sit on the porch and swing until about 8:45 PM. He would come inside and turn the TV off proclaiming that we had already seen that show. Of course, I never finished seeing the show, so I never knew how they ended. He had a natural gas upright heater in the far end of the house. He argued that he needed to go outside and get wood to put on the fire. It seemed cold to him. He could not understand that he no longer heated with coal and wood. He kept the house so hot that my sinuses got really dried out. I had not felt good since getting the flu.

He kept talking about raising a garden this year. This would only have made more work for us. He never helped with the garden when we were kids growing up. I never saw him pull any weeds for mom. He never put anything out to grow last year and I don't think he needs it as we were bringing his supper to him seven days a week. He only ate potatoes, tomatoes and occasionally he ate lettuce on a sandwich. I have tried making stews and he picks around the carrots. His eating habits changed after mom died and he retired.

As his demeanor changed, so did his health. He no longer could sleep for very long at night, slept the biggest portion of the day, and became very agitated if someone told him something might cost more than he thought it should have or if he didn't know exactly who his children were anymore, he might say things like, "Are you two married?" and it would be in reference to one of his children that had been married over 35 years. Some of the family didn't want to work together in his best interest. Special cameras were placed out of sight and without permission inside dad's home, accusations were made concerning theft of items form dad's that were unfounded, and when asked to write down about his day, what he ate, what his mood was like or what his conversation had been about, the request was ignored. Gossip among the family members and some of the community caused tension to escalate.

When dad started getting more aggressive and confused about who was there, why they were there, and constantly trying to leave, pounding his fists, etc. it was determined that we should check into what was available that would provide for his health needs, hygiene needs, and provide some peace of mind for the care givers.

Roger had power of attorney for dad and had gone through the courts and obtained guardianship of dad so he could make decisions for him. His truck and car both had been disabled and dad never even knew it. Roger, Ralph, and I started talking about what we should do. We decided to check out a nursing facility in London, Laurel Heights Nursing Home, and scheduled a time to visit the facility. As God worked this out, we went in and observed the patients, the workers, and the cleanliness of the facility. We were impressed and there happened to be an opening that day. That was a Friday. We decided to wait until Monday to schedule a meeting with the geriatric doctor and possibly admit dad. We took him, then stayed with him a few hours and proceeded to inform the other brother and sisters about the new direction. Seconds after I sent the text, I received a hateful message as a response and Facebook became flooded with negative remarks from those that had no idea what we really were dealing with. Dad was there in the nursing facility twelve days and died from a massive heart attack. It was his time to die, and I am so glad God worked this out that he died at the hospital where there were trained medical people to take care of him, instead of at home where I would have been the one scheduled to spend the night with him. He received the best care anyone could hope for and if he was really in his right mind, he would not have been a threat to himself. He was not in his right mind; therefore, this was the most we could do for him at home.

<u>Ephesians 6:2-3</u> — *"Honour thy father and mother; which is the first commandment with promise;"That it may be well with thee, and thou mayest live long on the earth*

CONVERSATION WITH DAD

I never really had much conversation with dad when I was growing up. I remember that most of our conversation was about work and how to complete a task without much help. We never really ever talked about things like what life had been about for my mom and him. Even when mom was alive, he was usually working during the day and resting during the evening. I recall him trying to help me learn subtraction when I was in the second grade. He could explain it in his way, but he got frustrated with me when I didn't pick up on it right away.

As he got older, in his early eighties, and his mental capacities had declined from the effects of Alzheimer's disease, he talked mostly about things that happened when he was about age seventeen to nineteen. I would ask him about things that had happened that day or the week before and he would give me a puzzled look. I might ask, even if I knew, who had been to see him that day, or if he went to the doctor, I might say, "What did your doctor think about you today?" He would not usually recall that he had been to the doctor that day or that anyone had visited him. I would ask if Diane came in over the weekend, when I knew she had, to see if he could remember. He would sometimes say, "If she did, I didn't see her." His conversation would usually be about his days of working in the coal mines in Harlan County, Kentucky.

His conversation would be, "Working in Harlan County was a good job. All the people that lived close by really tried to help your mom and me." He would then tell of how he would be able to come and visit his mom and dad, Russel, and Dora West, by getting a ride with a family that lived in Harlan County, always referred to as 'the Suttons'. He would recall they would sometimes come to Grandpa.

West's farm to hunt. My dad didn't have a driver's license at the time and didn't own a car, so they were happy to get a ride. They also rode a bus sometimes to Williamsburg, but he couldn't remember what the bus route covered.

I learned so much about dad after he was diagnosed with Alzheimer's disease. Many things I had never heard discussed before became new conversation. I had never heard mom or him speak about how they met. He remembered that and told that my mom's Uncle Earl Douglas was married to dad's first cousin, Joyce. His dad, my great grandfather, Alfred Douglas, enjoyed gospel music and often had 'singings' at his home. The whole community would come and partake in the singing and fellowship. Joyce was a first cousin to my dad. Earl invited dad to come to one of the singings and introduced my dad to my mom, Eula Mae Perkins.

I asked him about their life as they married, about a year after they met. He remarked that a man that he worked with had fallen on hard times and was going through a divorce. He owned a houseful of furniture. He offered to sell it to my dad for $200.00. They got everything from linens to bedroom sets to kitchen items. I questioned about how they got their belongings to Harlan since they owned no car. He said, "I guess we carried it in our arms. We didn't have anything much to carry, but I don't really remember."

They were married on May 21, 1949. Mom had just graduated from Pine Knot High School, in McCreary County, and dad had completed eighth grade at Fairview Elementary School, a one room school about a half mile from his home place. He talked about his first job that paid money. He worked in a sawmill, later in the mines, then carpenter work. Sometimes, dad would talk about the fish in his pond behind his house. He always invited us to go fishing but that wasn't possible because we had to be sure he wasn't near the pond because of his balance. His pond covered about two acres at the back of his property.

He would still laugh at things that we shared with him that were funny, but he couldn't repeat anything important that he should remember. When we finally had to have him placed in a nursing facility that cared for Alzheimer's patients 24 hours a day, he spoke with a social worker there a few days before he passed away. My brother Jerry, Kayla, my niece, and I were there visiting when they came to take him to talk with him. The nurse told me they had asked him a few questions. They asked him what year it was, and he answered, "It is 1966". They asked him who was the current president and he answered that "John F. Kennedy was the president". They asked him who was here visiting with him, and he answered "Carolyn, Louise, and Ralph." Louise passed away in 1994.

<u>Hebrews 9:27-28</u>— *And as it is appointed unto men once to die, but after this the judgment: So, Christ was once offered to bear the sins of many; and unto them that look for him shall he appear the second time without sin unto salvation.*

9-9-1991
Carolyn W. Reaves

Fall to Winter

Fall whispers its secret to the listening trees.
Soon everything dances to the gossipy breeze.
The leaves change their colors and scatter on the ground.
They wither to nothingness and can't be found.

The windows become canvases for the frost.
Etching marks on the panes and becoming embossed.
The leaves crackle as they begin to break.
With very few chances left to take.

The pumpkins glow with faces full of light.
Frosty panes glisten on chilly nights.
Fall can't keep the secrets anymore.
Winter arrives to tell us more.

9-4-1991
Dealing With Loss
Carolyn W. Reaves

Dealing With Loss

The seasons come and the seasons go.
I painfully still miss you so.
The leaves have fallen and the snow is gone.
The pain from your leaving lingers on.

Spring faithfully arrived with all its glory,
Bringing with it Summer's story.
Seeds were sown and the fields did provide.
Our tears and sorrow we cannot hide.

I see your beauty in the flowers that bloom.
Faded roses remind me of the gloom.
I'm reminded of how short a life span really is,
And how much is taken for granted in the life we live.

Trying to make good memories each passing day.
Looking for the good in every possible way.
One day I will be gone and you will forever miss me
Toss all your pain and sorrow into the sea.

10-11-1991
Carolyn W. Reaves

Between Life and Death

Getting older once seemed so far away.
Now, looking back it seems like only yesterday.
Memories of childhood play tricks on my mind,
Making me believe those lost years I'll again find.

There's a fine line between life and death,
From the first time and the last time we take a breath.
Lots of love, happiness, sorrow, and tears
Are filled into spaces between the years.

None knows the day or the final hour
When we meet our Maker in all His power.
Life is a gift given from God above
Our feelings take shape in the form of love.

The Face
10-11-1991
Carolyn W. Reaves

The Face

The face tells all secrets and will not lie.

It tells when you are happy and when you cry.

The face hides lots of thoughts, but tells even more.

It reveals our feelings and leads us to explore.

It arouses curiosity and causes us to listen.

It expresses our emotions and makes eyes glisten.

The face shows anger when no words are even spoken.

It reveals happiness, giving a smile as a token.

Expressions on the face you cannot hide,

Even if you have thoughts and feelings hidden deep inside.

I Remember

I remember when I was very young
Going to church and the songs that were sung.
I remember hearing the piano play
And I recall hearing people pray.

I remember my grandmother as the Sunday School Teacher
Always trying to be a Christian and Soul Reacher.
The revivals would begin in the Spring of the year
The evangelist spent the week at their farm that was near.

The farm had lots to consider, but not one complained
As there was always plenty to eat and the
family was entertained
By the preacher as he read from the Book
And told them of how Jesus
made a way for any that would look.

His ways are a mystery and some things we just take by faith
But believing is the way to escape
Eternal burning in the fiery lake.
I remember the night I gave my heart to the Lord.
I poured my heart out as I could not find words
To express what I felt in my heart that night
As his voice I heard say, "Child, everything is all right".

I remember…

Think for Today

Today started like all the rest.

I prepared to challenge the class with a test.

Many had studied and read their book

Some had not even given it a look.

They paid for the course, but didn't try

They waited until test day and then they cried.

With excuse after excuse about what went wrong.

Some can make the whine turn it into a song.

Losing is easy if that is what you must do.

Thinking never hurt anyone and that is true.

Spring on its Way

The sign pointed to Spring, just go ahead and enter.
I couldn't go yet, because I am cold and lazy Winter.
My snow is still sleeping on the cold, cold ground.
But daffodils are now peeking up and looking around.
As the days get longer and the sun shines so bright,
I realize it is time for me to take my annual flight.
I'll take white blankets and cover the tall pine trees,
And watch children play and the sleds crawl over me.
I'll be back to visit after Summer begins to fade,
And again cover the mountains with beautiful cascades.

Carolyn Reaves 10/24/2018

My Dad and How He Lived

Twenty-Eight years went by, and he never once called. I wondered if my phone number he ever recalled. As time went by and his short-term memory began to fade, I cherished the memories from my childhood more each day. Some memories were of times when we all enjoyed a meal together.

We spent lots of time inside in rainy or snowy weather. I remember how he wore his hat when he went outside. And days he went fishing with his two oldest boys while I stayed behind. He and mom used to sit on the porch swing and talk every summer night, their conversation would end when the mosquitos started to bite. I never recalled hearing conversation about how those two first met.

One day, when his long-term memory was good, I asked, and this is what he said: "Your Great-Grandpa, Alfred Douglas, enjoyed gospel singing at his home. Your Great Uncle, Earl Douglas, invited me and he asked me if I would like to go along." "I went and that's how it started—we would go to church and sit together in the pew." He said, "She was a good woman and I miss her, and I know you kids do, too." Now this journey he started on has come to an abrupt and final end. I know he is with mom now and all his long-forgotten family and friends.

Carolyn Reaves

MY FAMILY

The things I am proudest of are my life experiences and the family God has allowed me to be a part of. God placed me with a wonderful spouse. Anthony is one of the kindest, most caring men I have ever known. He is a Christian and his love for Christ is evident in his daily life. He works hard and is devoted to working for the Lord. He serves as a pastor of Red Bird Baptist Church. He has served as a bi-vocational pastor, but recently retired from his job working in the technology department in McCreary County Schools I came from a family of eight children; Anthony has no brothers, but he has one sister, Cheryl.

Our backgrounds are different in many ways, but we help each other. Clarissa and Herbert live in Cookeville, TN. and Angelina lives here in Kentucky. Both of them are very independent ladies that have a genuine concern for their country, their family, and for their fellow man. I am confident that they could find a solution to their problems by praying and reading their Bible.

Our grandchildren have blessed us with their lives and continue to do so. Kiersten, our eldest grandchild, is married to Gage Bowlin. They now have four children. Maxtyn Gage Anthony Bowlin is their eldest child. He was a miracle as far as we can tell. They prayed for this child to be a part of their lives and God worked this out for them.

Bethany, our second eldest grandchild, is a very artistic, young lady with lots of ambition to become absorbed in doing digital marketing. She has skills for working with the community, computer knowledge, and lives in Florida, by choice. She is the daughter of Clarissa and Herbert Williams, Jr. Cameron, our eldest grandson, enjoys video games, is in college now, and is preparing for a bright future. He enjoys spending time with us sometimes during the summer and has helped me several times with gardening and harvesting our vegetables. He and Bethany were both baptized in the ocean when their family all lived in Florida.

Carlee is a blond, blue-eyed girl, full of energy and giggles. She enjoys crafts, painting, cooking, and playing with "slime" that she has made or bought. She has given us several pictures she has drawn, and we cherish them all. Some become refrigerator art, and some go into a file with her name on it.

She is now a cheerleader, able to do several cheers involving tumbling, mounts and other skills.

Rafe is the brown-eyed, smiling, smart boy that likes to wear white t-shirts and bibbed overalls because they are comfortable. He loves making things with Legos, especially complicated ones.

Justice is the blue-eyed girl that smiles constantly and loves learning whatever Rafe is doing in school. She is doing well in school and enjoys learning. She always tells me all they do at school is have fun. I think she likes going to school so much that it seems like all of it is fun. When she and Rafe were very young, their favorite thing to do was go on a "Treasure hunt". I have a bowl that sits gracefully in my living room filled with pretty rocks, pinecones, buckeyes, and feathers.

I also have four great grandchildren. I know they are excited and will love the new addition to their family. Maxtyn is 3, Harvey is 2, Tobias is almost 12 months old, and Clementine is about 4 weeks old. They love playing outside, helping in the vegetable garden, gathering eggs from the henhouse. There is never a dull moment.

Carolyn West Reaves

Who's the Girl in the Mirror? Revisited

QUARANTINED AND FACING A FUNERAL

Working on a large farm in rural Kentucky was considered a way of life for many in this area. The farm, which consisted of about two hundred acres, relied on every family member to help with the general operations. The children were all young and Grandma West was pregnant with her youngest son, Charles.

She had given birth to nine healthy children and was pregnant with her 10th child when one of her sons was diagnosed with Polio. This was her six-year- old son, Lonnie. He had been a playful young boy, enrolled in school and suddenly became ill with this terrible disease that Grandma and Grandpa couldn't find relief in.

They took him to the doctor, and he was sent back home to be taken out of school and nobody was allowed to visit for fear of being infected. The health department ordered signs to be placed on the property "QUARANTINED – DO NOT ENTER". Polio was still a very aggressive viral type of disease that had not been treated successfully with vaccines at this time. This was in January 1936. School had just ended for this term and just a few short weeks earlier, Lonnie had participated in the Christmas play at school. What was once a healthy, energetic child was now fighting for his life. He was described as the weakest he had ever been and could no longer walk. After the diagnosis made by the local doctor, Doctor West, Lonnie only lived for four days and required constant care, which was aided by his older brothers and sisters. A funeral was planned but Grandma was too sick to attend his funeral. She was six months pregnant and the thought of burying one of her children was almost unbearable for her. Two of their older daughters had to stay home with Grandma during the funeral because she was pregnant and grief from losing Lonnie could possibly cause her to lose this child, too. A man by the name of Ed Smith dug the grave for the family at Alsile Baptist Church, which is a couple of miles from their farm.

There were no phones in the community and communication amongst the neighbors was very minor due to the quarantine. The other children were having to deal with a new problem, that of giving up their brother. They had fond memories of playing together on the big farm and watching Lonnie perform in the school play as Tiny Tim. Not really knowing anything about Polio, my dad, age 7 at the time, and Marie, age 9, found comfort in listening to records grandpa ordered for them to play on the old crank style victrola. They just assumed that they were all going to die, and they figured a funeral would be planned for them, too.

They had made special music selections and decided upon these in case there should be another child in the family suddenly passed away. The music they planned for their funerals where two songs from the records grandpa had purchased. For Marie, age 9, she picked out "I Just Came to Get My Baby Out of Jail" and my father, age 7 at the time, picked out "I'm Just a Hen-Pecked Man."

Lonnie was the only child in the family that got Polio and died. This had to have been one of the hardest things my grandmother had to endure during her pregnancy. I never heard my dad talk about losing his brother but my aunt Marie, now 94, enjoyed telling me about this bit of family history.

If I had known about this funeral selection made by dad when he was then 7 years old, I would have had this song played at dad's funeral in 2018.

ACKNOWLEDGEMENT

I want to thank the teachers that inspired me to learn and keep trying to do my best. I affectionately remember **Ms. Emma Dame** in Flat Rock, Michigan for teaching me to work independently and to have a vision for doing all I could for myself. I also want to thank my elementary teachers at Jellico Creek Elementary School, especially **Mrs. Gladys Meadors, and Mrs. Letha H. Taylor**. They did excellent teaching, even though we had very little to work with other than what teachers bought themselves or parents brought in for the students. I extend a special thank you to **Mrs. Emma Sharp,** one of my high school English teachers, for inspiring me to become a teacher. All of these lead by example and even though I cannot personally thank each of them now as most of my teachers are no longer here, I extend a thank you in memory of them.

I also want to thank my husband for encouragement and his willingness to read and offer his suggestions for improvement in this writing. I sincerely appreciate the time he spent reading it. I thank each of my daughters for providing me with many pages of writing material so that my book was more than five pages.

Thanks to those that have offered up prayers for my family and me during our times of grief. Funerals are never easy but knowing that a church family would pray and keep you in their thoughts was very comforting. I have enjoyed hearing the testimonies from those that have lost their loved ones. Testimonies of those already gone still come back to me at times when I feel especially lonely and sad. God's faithful remnant have proven to be there through all of my trials.

I also thank an anonymous letter writer for the comments. I will just say that every person on this earth has pages they don't want others to read. When I got saved, Jesus was the cover for all my mistakes and sins. He has torn those pages out. I want to thank Jesus Christ for His gifts and the working for Him.

www.ingramcontent.com/pod-product-compliance
Lightning Source LLC
LaVergne TN
LVHW040152080526
838202LV00042B/3130